CW00670608

Twice-Told Tales

The Psychological Use of Fairy Tales

HANS DIECKMANN

Foreword by Bruno Bettelheim

Translated by Boris Matthews

CHIRON PUBLICATIONS • **Wilmette, Illinois**

Originally published in 1978 as *Gelebte Märchen*
Copyright 1979, Gerstenberg Verlag

© **1986** by Chiron Publications. All rights reserved. No part of
this publication may be reproduced, stored in a retrieval
system, or transmitted, in any form by any means, electronic,
mechanical, photocopying, recording, or otherwise, without
the prior written permission of the publisher,
Chiron Publications, 400 Linden Avenue,
Wilmette, Illinois 60091

Translation © 1986 by Chiron Publications
Library of Congress Catolog Card Number: 86-2625

Book design by Elaine M. Hill
Printed in the United States of America

Library of Congress Cataloging-in-Publication Data
Dieckmann, Hans.
Twice-told tales.

Translation of: Gelebte Märchen.
Includes index.
1. Fairy tales—Psychological aspects. 2. Fairy
tales—Therapeutic use. 3. Symbolism (Psychology).
4. Fantasy. 5. Psychotherapy. I. Title.
RC489.F3D5413 1986   616.89′14   86-2625
ISBN 0-933029-02-0

Second printing, 1989

Contents

Foreword

Fairy tales are often central in the dreams of adults, just because of the important role they played in their childhood psychic life. Fairy tales commonly occupy much of the small child's mind; the child weaves fantasies around them, integrates fairy-tale motifs into play and daydreams, and acts the stories out with puppets or with friends. Fairy-tale figures give children someone to identify with; they may see themselves as the hero who slays the dragon, or as Simpleton who in the end proves his superiority to his clever brothers, who then are revealed as being the true simpletons. Or the child may identify with much-abused Cinderella, who in the end triumphs over her evil sisters, or with Beauty, who restores the Beast to his true humanity and in the process saves her father and puts her jealous sisters into their places. And where is the child who, even if she or he does not identify with Hansel or Gretel, fails to rejoice in their overcoming the evil witch, and who at Christmastime does not happily nibble on the gingerbread house, this symbol of how children can get the better of a threatening, evil old woman?

Children's fantasies based on fairy tales are an extremely important element in their psychic lives, not least because of the dangers these tales describe, which have much in common with the young child's basic anxieties—such as those of abandonment, mistreatment, being belittled, or being threatened by ogres or wild animals. The fairy tale's obligatory happy ending assures children that despite all their anxieties, they eventu-

Copyright © 1985 by Bruno Bettelheim

ally will be victorious. Such messages help children to manage hardships in their lives, whether real or imagined.

Since fairy tales have such significance in the minds of children, it is easy to understand why fairy-tale motifs continue to play important roles in the conscious, but more frequently and dominantly in the unconscious of adults, even when they feel they have largely forgotten the tale and its importance for them.

The great contribution of this very interesting book by Dieckmann is that it demonstrates for the first time that some persons do act out fairy tales in their lives. The case histories presented here amply show that there can be deep-reaching connections between a child's favorite fairy tale and his or her fate later in life; the fairy-tale motifs become formative elements of the personality, for better or for worse. Usually completely unknown to the persons, these motifs so influence individuals' views of themselves and of their world that they are induced to act them out in life. Dieckmann here shows the importance fairy tales can have in the treatment of adults, and, further, how they can actually dominate people's psychic lives.

Dieckmann, being a Jungian psychoanalyst, relies mainly on Jungian interpretations of fairy tales; they can equally well be understood from a Freudian perspective. But what is truly important is the demonstration that a child's favorite fairy tale can continue to play a significant role in his or her life whether or not the adult is aware of it. This book demonstrates how such an influence can be made to cure pathological processes. Fortunately, however, in the lives of most poeple, fairy tales serve much more positive goals. As Dieckmann states at the end of his book: "Only he acquires wisdom who also experienced deeply the dark aspects of our humanity."

Freud began his 1913 essay on fairy-tale topics in dreams by stating that it is hardly surprising to learn from psychoanalysis about the great importance fairy tales have in the psychic life of children. He continues with the observation that for some adults, their favorite childhood fairy tale has taken the place of some of their childhood memories. In such cases the stories have become cover memories, which hide repressed events of considerable significance.

Freud also remarked that elements and situations derived from fairy tales appear frequently in the dreams of adults. Typically, in the process of interpreting such dreams, other pertinent parts of the tale come to mind and permit a better understanding of the dream, and of why this particular tale has special meaning to the dreamer. To illustrate all this Freud describes how in the analysis of two of his patients, some of the Brothers

Grimm's fairy tales played a significant role. In one case it was the story of "Rumpelstiltskin"; in the other, a combination of two tales, "The Wolf and the Seven Little Kids" and "Little Red Cap." In the latter instance, the patient and his analysis became famous as the case of the Wolfman, named after the patient's involvement with these tales.

Fairy tales are so important because they can help us cope with the dark sides of ourselves—sometimes in deviant ways, as was true for some of the patients whose cases are presented in this book. They also can influence our lives in positive ways.

In teaching psychology to graduate students, I found it useful for my purposes and meaningful to the students to ask them to remember a fairy tale that had been important to them in their childhood. I asked them to retell this story in writing as they recalled it, and to reflect on why they thought this particular tale might have been significant to them. Nearly all students could remember at least one such story, and most of them had some idea why it might have taken hold of their imagination.

After the students had written this assignment, I then asked them to reread the tale in question and then write an essay observing how it had become altered in their memory of it, while considering what this distortion in their memory could reveal about the significance this tale had for them and perhaps continued to have for them. It turned out that every one of these very intelligent students had originally been convinced that they had recollected their story true to the original version. It was quite a revelation to them to discover how much, in fact, their memories had distorted the story. Not only were the students' versions of these stories quite different from the originals, but in many cases the story as recalled was a combination of two or more different stories. In other instances, random figures or events had in memory become elevated to central importance; and in some cases, the tale as remembered was in important elements exactly opposite to the original version.

In speculating how and why they remembered these stories in so different a form, many students comprehended, either for the first time or much more fully, why this particular story had been so important to them. Further, they often discovered that only the changes they had made in the story permitted them to find great personal significance in it. Only in a distorted form had the story fit the problem which had beset them at the time or offered a much desired solution to a pressing problem. This is why only in its altered form had the story become memorable, and in some cases it remained significant in their lives right up to the present.

Asked to recall her favorite childhood fairy tale, one student, a normal,

well-functioning person in her mid-twenties, wrote instead a diatribe
against what she characterized as male chauvinism in "Hansel and Gretel."
The story had obsessed her as a child and had continued to make her very
angry whenever it came to her mind, which happened frequently. She explained in her essay that what made her furious about this well-known and
popular fairy tale was that the girl was described as nothing but an empty-
headed tag-along to her brother; that she was always doing his bidding
without a thought of her own. In her memory, Hansel completely dominated Gretel and the story by doing everything, like laying out the pebbles
and later the bread crumbs to make it possible for the children to return
home, and saving them in the end by his daring act of pushing the witch
into the oven and burning her to death. Hansel did it all, while Gretel just
sat passively in the cage, doing nothing to save herself. This story had been
and still was very important to this woman, because it was in many ways
the story of *her* life, which had been and still was entirely dominated by her
brother, a few years older than she. The story enraged her because it im-
plied that girls on their own can do nothing, and it obviously induced girls
to accept this passive role as their fate in life, as had been the case for her.
This woman ended her essay by saying that even now, as she was about to
receive her master's degree, she still relied on her brother, who was in an
entirely different field of work, to tell her what work to apply for. She in
large part blamed this dependency on fairy tales such as this one, which
she felt impressed girls with the message that domination by older brothers—or males—is their inescapable lot.

When the next assignment required this woman to reread the fairy tale,
she was dumbfounded to discover—contrary to what had been her clear
recollection of the story—that it is Gretel who pushes the witch into the
oven, thus saving herself, and Hansel who all the while is sitting helplessly
in the cage. This woman was certain that in her childhood she had known
only the story as she had recalled it all through the years up to now, a story
which had always filled her with anger. Convinced that there must have
been a version of "Hansel and Gretel" as *she* recalled it, she searched for
days in all available libraries to find *her* story, and questioned her friends
and various authorities in the hope of finding someone who knew it.

Finally it dawned on her that it had been she who had seen herself all
along in the role of a poor Gretel, one who had helplessly let herself be put
into the cage to passively await her end, one who would have perished
had not Hansel managed to push the witch into the oven and thus liberate
them both, a feat for which Gretel owed him eternal obedience. In re-

sponse to this truly revealing discovery, the student made a serious effort to understand why this distortion had taken place in her memory, and why it had continued to haunt her.

To her complete surprise, she found that a traumatic event during her teenage years provided the clue for a deeper understanding of why she had to believe that it had been Hansel who had burned the witch. When this woman had been still a teenager, her mother—a devout Catholic—had suddenly died. Her brother was abroad at the time and could not return for the funeral. In discussing with him by telephone how things ought to be arranged, the brother had suggested that their mother should be cremated. Although this was only a suggestion, and although this girl knew that her mother would have wanted to have been buried, she took, as always, any suggestion by her brother as an order to be obeyed, and so she arranged for her mother's cremation. But she had felt very guilty about it, and so she had contrived in her unconscious to make herself innocent of thus going against her mother's wishes. To convince herself that any cremation could only be the result of someone else's action, she had changed in her mind the story of Hansel and Gretel so that it was the brother who had burned the old woman.

In finally recognizing how she had distorted this important story, the student realized that all along she had also distorted her relation to her brother. It had not been her brother who had forced her to do always as he wanted, it had been she herself who had seen him as her absolute master. Because she had needed to believe it was her brother who was responsible for her mother's cremation so that she would not need to feel guilty about it, she had made her brother into her god and master, one who made her decisions, so that she would never have to feel responsible, or possibly guilty, about anything she did.

As so often with children and their favorite fairy tale, the story of Hansel and Gretel had served this student well, albeit only in its distorted form. It had provided justification for living a passive role which, while often uncomfortable, had provided complete protection against all guilt. By taking on the role of Gretel *as she perceived it*, this student had not only permitted but invited her brother to run her life for her. However, in consequence, none of this student's real accomplishments, such as her success in college and in her graduate studies, had given her any satisfaction. Her actions did not give her a feeling of being an independent person, since despite them she always felt hopelessly outclassed by her brother. She saw herself as a "victim."

Now she recognized that this dependent posture had been her own doing, as had been the role she had assigned to Gretel in the story. As she realized it all and was writing the second assignment, she interrupted her task to call her brother; she told him that she decided to apply for a different job from the one he had suggested. To her great surprise and elation, he congratulated her on being finally able to make her own decisions and went on to tell her what a relief this was to him, who had felt her dependency on him as a heavy burden. With that, she decided that from now on she would take her fate into her own hands, as Gretel had really done in the story.

This example is given to suggest that living out to some degree features of one's favorite childhood fairy tale can serve positive purposes. In this case, this fairy tale as remembered offered the student an excuse for living in dependence on an older, dominant brother, while anger at the story and its male chauvinism preserved the girl's sanity. A couple of years later this young woman let me know that her life had indeed become changed. Even so, the tale had not become unimportant to her, because in its true form it continued to be a mainstay of her life. Whenever she became discouraged, she reminded herself that as Gretel had been able to save herself and her brother, she herself could perform well, too. Thus for her, there was finally a happy ending to her story of Hansel and Gretel.

So, too, with the cases Dieckmann narrates, since through his sensitive understanding and appreciation of the importance of favorite childhood fairy tales, he has been able to cure many patients.

Bruno Bettelheim

Author's Preface to the
American Edition

After completing my training, I was active a long time in internal medicine. It was a great experience during my training in analytical psychology to again encounter in medical psychology the shapes of fantasy from fairy tale and myth which had occupied me so intensely during my childhood and youth and which, at that time, I had read and reread with much enthusiasm. If one is not a creative artist, the so-called rational adult life and the rationality of modern professions all too easily let one forget precisely this realm from childhood; thus the world loses a piece of its colorfulness and its mystery.

I cannot really say that, during my first years of activity as an analyst, fairy tales stood in the forefront of my interest, but rather that I ran up against them in my patients. In many of my adult patients I discovered the very great influence that their favorite childhood fairy tale had exerted on them and still exerted in their unconscious (I describe this in more detail in Chapter 5). In Germany, my first explorations of this theme met with lively interest, an interest that ultimately led me to report on this topic in a major paper at one of the international congresses for analytical psychology. This paper also stimulated interest in this theme among American colleagues, and toward the end of the 1960s I was invited to America to talk about it.

When I told my European colleagues of my invitation and of my intention to speak about fairy tales in America, I was met with great skepticism. They objected that American children and also the present generation of American adults had had scarcely anything at all to do with fairy tales, but rather had grown up with the movies about Mickey Mouse, Donald Duck, Superman, etc. Of course at first this considerably shook my confidence, and I began to peruse a whole series of these comics in which, to be sure, I found that they also contained magical, mythological motifs such as occur in fairy tales, but that they were rather far removed from the motifs and motif patterns of the usual, authentic folk fairy tale. Just to be safe, I worked a few references to this into my manuscript.

And so somewhat uneasily I flew to New York and expected to find only a tiny audience of European immigrants who could warm to this theme. So much the greater was my astonishment when in New York I spoke on this topic to a great hall overflowing with several hundred persons. My talk was followed by extraordinarily lively discussion that evidenced the same interest I had already encountered in Europe. This phenomenon was repeated in all the other American cities where I spoke on this topic. It became clear to me that the German poet Hauff was absolutely correct when he maintained that fairy tales possess a fascination across the centuries of human development, independent of all historical currents and cultures, which makes them ineradicable and that every generation takes them up anew in order to delight in them and to occupy themselves with them. When I returned from this first visit to the United States, I had very clearly altered my image of America, and through the medium of the fairy tale I had gotten a very clear sense of how stupid many of the collective European prejudices were. Then many years later in the United States Bruno Bettelheim's world-famous book, *The Uses of Enchantment,* appeared confirming my experience of the necessity and the importance of fairy tales and fairy-tale motifs in the development of the human psyche. For this reason I am very grateful that he has written a Foreword to this book.

Aside from one chapter of this book that treats the influence of the fairy tale on the psychic development of the child, my studies have focused predominantly on adult patients and on those processes in the magico-mythological layer of the human unconscious which, as we know today, has not only negative-irrational effects on the conscious but is also the wellspring of creative innovations and of deep transformative processes. Although as examples I have, of course, dealt primarily with European fairy tales corresponding to the case material that was available to me, I do hope that this book, which has aroused interest in the German language area for several years, will find a friendly, interested reception among the American public. Fairy-tale motifs illustrating the archetypal structures of human psychic development are, of course, such universals that we meet the same motifs everywhere in the world. Human creative fantasy brings forth these same motifs, regardless of the culture, as all modern research in this area has shown.

Hans Dieckmann

Author's Preface to the First Edition

Since the small pocket edition of *Märchen und Träume als Helfer des Menschen*, which first appeared in 1966, has been out of print for some time after three editions, it seemed appropriate to revise the material thoroughly and to bring it up to date. I am indebted to the Gerstenberg Verlag for giving me the opportunity to revise these texts and to alter and substantially expand them.

Chapter 3, containing a detailed interpretation of the beloved tale of Hansel and Gretel—the "standard German fairy tale"—was added. (This is a revised version of "Der Wert des Märchens fü die seelische Entwicklung des Kindes," which appeared in *Praxis der Kinderpsychologie und Kinderpsychiatrie*, Feb.–March 1966.) This relates to the process of development and maturation in the child and is particularly relevant from the viewpoint of depth psychology. It expands on the very brief interpretation from Chapter 1, important in the psychology of the child, a chapter which got short shrift in the original text.

In place of the very terse paragraph concerning the favorite fairy tale from childhood in the old Chapter 2, there is now a full, comprehensive chapter with a number of case examples. This is intended to give a brief overview of my research, which up until now has been published in numerous scattered journal articles and which has been taken up in various places, including America, where Berne and his school have dealt with it. Indeed, I plan an extensive publication thoroughly discussing the entire empirical experience of this area, but it will still take a number of years to complete. Hence it seemed appropriate here to include this theme as a chapter:

the extent to which people live out such mythologems in every detail, and what considerable influence these background images have on peoples' ways of experiencing and behaving. This theme belongs among the most astonishing experiences of my analytic activity. This holds true not only in the ego-formation of severely disturbed patients, but also for the so-called healthy individuals.

Furthermore, Chapter 4, concerning the problem of cruelty in fairy tales, is new. (It is a revised version of "Zum Aspekt des Grausamen im Märchen," in *Praxis der Kinderpsychologie und Kinderpsychiatrie*, November/December 1967.) This problem in particular always takes the foreground in discussions of fairy tales, and it seems important to me that it be treated not only by pedagogues, poets, psychologists, philosophers, and scholars but by analysts of the human unconscious as well since it is precisely this theme that is so closely linked with the extraordinarily important question of early human attempts at managing aggression. This chapter also includes a case example referring to the favorite childhood fairy tale and hence is not limited to theoretical debates but rather presents this problem concretely, using the experience and transformations of an individual human being.

Through these additions the book has grown to almost twice its original size. The remaining old text was revised, enlarged, and also cut in places, so that basically a new book came into being, which, I hope, will also be interesting and new to the reader who already knows the earlier version. These considerations seemed to justify the title *Twice-Told Tales*, which is intended to point out how much emotionally and practically important truth there is in these products of human fantasy that we call fairy tales and often devalue.

On the one hand, this book is a source of information for the layperson interested in this topic, but on the other it is a first, elementary, and brief introduction for the physician and psychologist working analytically. The book contains graphic depictions of the form in which fairy-tale material arises within the analytic process, how it can be treated and how it can be fruitfully and usefully worked through in the therapeutic process to the benefit of the patient—be it child or adult.

My especial thanks go to Martin Oesch at Gerstenberg Verlag, the publisher, to my wife for many ideas and suggestions, and to my secretary Sigrid Wiegand for the extra typing.

Berlin   *Hans Dieckmann*
December 1977

CHAPTER 1

Fairy Tale and Dream

There is a famous Indian fairy tale collection of stories within a story. The outer story begins with the account of a magician who appears each day in the king's audience hall and gives the king an apple. Each time the king unmindfully hands it on to his vizier, who has it thrown into an out-of-the-way chamber. This goes on for an entire year until one day the queen's ape, who has broken loose, leaps into the king's audience hall, seizes the apple, and bites into it. As he does so, all present see, to their amazement, that this apple contains a marvelously beautiful jewel at its core. Now, of course, the king immediately finds out where the other apples are and has his chamberlain look. And in fact under the rotted flesh of the apples lies a pile of valuable gems, exactly as many as there are days in the year.

This is similar to the way we treat fairy tales. After our childhood we usually throw them away as worthless. "Only a fairy tale," we say, and let it decay in some out-of-the-way chamber. Until, that is, a situation perhaps arises—be it a severe emotional illness or a life crisis—in which we open this chamber of necessity. Here, too, we could say, it molders because all these years we have not been concerned with its content. When Freud began to concern himself with unconscious fantasies, he wrote in his book on dreams the sentence: *Flectere si nequeo superos,/Acheronta movebo*—"If I cannot bend the gods, I will move the underworld." Among the contaminated fantasies in this underworld we often find the gems of deep wisdom and the symbols and motifs, not only of the fairy tales of our own childhood, but those of all humanity.

The depth psychological interpretation of fairy tales and myths arose ini-

1

tially as a necessity in the treatment of neuroses. As is generally known, dreams and their interpretation by the doctor are an important factor in the therapy of emotionally ill persons. Freud had already seen that fairy tales and myths do not differ fundamentally from dreams and that they speak the same symbolic language. Again and again mythological material turns up in the dreams of our patients and compels us to seek a way of understanding it. Here especially the work of C. G. Jung and his school has pointed the way. But just as the dream is a universal human phenomenon that visits both the healthy and the ill, so, too, are myths and fairy tales universal phenomena. Understanding their symbolism in the case of an emotionally ill person who has gotten stuck in certain maturational processes and sees himself faced with unsolvable problems simultaneously opens the path to understanding the common language of mythologems, that is, the typical patterns we find in myth. Those suffering from neuroses are not entirely different people with entirely different problems from the rest of us; they have the same human problems and difficulties. They differ from the healthy person only in that, thanks to definite inner and outer givens, they cannot solve their problems alone.

This book is written less from the rigorously categorizing and abstractly evaluating view of rational science than from the joy and interest in the magnificent, colorful, many-sided fantasy world of fairy tales which the collective unconscious of mankind for thousands of years has brought forth always and again. Their power to give form and their wisdom have never entirely released me from their grip since I first came in contact with their richness as a small boy at my grandmother's house. Again they came very much alive when I began to tell them to my first child, and finally I found all these beloved friends of my childhood again in the unconscious of my patients when I became a psychoanalyst. In the consciousness of my patients they were often long forgotten; but there in the unconscious they still lived. They rose up in my patients' dreams and told them many strange things they had never paid attention to, things that they had always passed by, and which now suddenly revealed themselves as the greatest of treasures of the soul. The fairy tales often gave them insights that could give color and vivacity to a life grown empty, sterile, and desolate.

This language in which fairy tales and myths speak to us out of our own unconscious is one I would miss more than the cleverest rational theory of science. As an instrument for treating my emotionally ill patients it has given me endless riches, and not at all infrequently a fairy tale and the insights we have drawn from its deeper significance have become the central element in treatment. What transpires between doctor and patient in this sort of encounter cannot be described in its ultimate and deepest significance. It remains beyond what words can grasp: unique and irreplaceable. It is one of the most profound impressions of my professional experience that the right story at the right place and right time and which precisely grasps the patient's problem can form a bridge between two people.

CHAPTER **2**

The Symbolic Language of Fairy Tales

"Once upon a time . . . ." So begin most of our fairy tales, and then they take us far back into a distant, long-forgotten time in which strange things happen—impossible, according to the rational mind—a time in which monsters exist, and witches, fairies, and magicians, or talking animals. It is a world full of miracles in which a swineherd becomes a king, Cinderella becomes a princess, the water of life can be found, a lamp can magically produce all the treasures, a ring can give the power to rule the world, or a horse can bear one aloft. There is scarcely one among us who did not grow up with these stories, for whom they were not the first and earliest encounter with the creative, shaping fantasy of our culture.

Regardless of how much we clung to these stories and heard or read them again and again as children, later in life we tended to lay them aside with a disparaging comment. The phrase "only a fairy tale" often carries the negative accent of fantastic invention or even fraud. Scarcely one of our average adults today would muster the interest and the patience of King Shahrirar to listen for a thousand and one nights to the stories of a Scheherazade, although that appears to have agreed with him very well; for what he thought was long lost—love, trust, and human relatedness —he again found in this way. "Oh, King! Such legends are full of secret meaning known only to the initiated," says Scheherazade at the end of one of the tales she tells. But we usually know either nothing or very little about it.

In our life, too, in our reality, there is that "once upon a time." Each of us had a time in which new and wondrous things happened almost daily.

Think about it: Everything the adult takes for granted every day had once upon a time to be newly discovered and acquired by the child. What an endless number of new acquisitions were made in childhood! All this indeed "happens miraculously." Scarcely one among us can still summon up the feelings that filled us when we took the first steps upright; but most of us probably still know how we felt when we could swim or ride a bicycle for the first time. Whenever one reaches out to something new, something until now either unknown or impossible, and makes it one's own, something happens that is like the transition of the fairy-tale hero from the everyday world into a bewitched, unknown, magical realm that must be set free, or from which something of value must be fetched which enriches everyday life. Then the witches and monsters are our own personified anxieties and ineptitudes with which we must do battle; the helpful animals and the fairies are abilities and possibilities yet unknown to us which can accrue to us in such situations. Thus what is image or fantasy in the fairy tale becomes reality on another level.

These always vital new acquisitions and new creations, however, which occur in childhood in such profusion that we would not exaggerate if we called the child "polymorphously genial," never completely cease to appear in the course of a healthily flowing life. To the extent that we do not petrify in an empty routine, which, alas, all too often does occur, it happens again and again that we experience a fairy tale and the "miraculous" enters our life as something new and, until now, totally unknown. In every human existence there are great, generally valid stations on the path of life where such things must take place: after a phase of infantile dependency on the mother, every human being experiences the first autonomy and separation in the phase of defiance, everyone also experiences the awakening of sexuality in puberty and the necessity of relating to the opposite sex. The challenges of midlife confront everybody when life begins to decline and should move more in the direction of depth rather than breadth, and every life ends in death, with its problem of the transition into another world or another form of existence of which we know nothing.

Whenever we stand confronted with such new and often frightening situations, first of all we attempt to form an image or picture, a picture of the possibilities of how it might be, of how we might master the new conditions, of what tasks are to be mastered and what dangers overcome. Here the collective, traditional images can help us. If we know how to understand them rightly, they express in their symbols something about how mankind has always done it or could do it. The language of these images is many layered and ultimately inexhaustible like any genuine symbol, like every spontaneously appearing carrier of meaning, which makes it possible to represent contents that are representable in no other way. Thus we can understand a fairy tale on many levels. The psychological element, too, is only a part of the possible content, and in each phase of life a symbol can manifest an additional, concrete content. Thus it gains a new and deepened meaning and enlarges our understanding.

Snake Fairy Tales

Let us see what that means in terms of a real fairy tale. As an example let us take the fairy tale of a prince who was changed into a snake, or was actually born as a snake; then, through the love of a maiden, he is set free. This fairy tale exists in our cultural field in various versions, including one in *German Fairy Tales Since Grimm* (Zaunert, ed., 1964), a Swedish version (von der Leyen and Zaunert, eds., 1922), an Albanian tale (von Massenbach, ed., 1985), and a Greek island fairy tale (Karlinger, ed., 1960). I will tell it from the Greek.

Greek Version

> Once there was a merchant who had three daughters. One day before he set out on his travels, he asked them what he should bring them. The oldest wanted a petticoat, the second jewelry, and the youngest nothing but a few roses which just now were plentiful and cheap. The merchant concluded his business and bought the presents for his daughters. On his way home, he got into a hail storm which tore the petals from the roses; finally he found shelter in a deserted castle. Food stood on the table, and he ate of it; and at the gate there was a rose bush from which he picked a new bouquet for his daughter. At that very moment a snake appeared and demanded of him that he bring his youngest daughter in exchange for its beloved roses. The frightened merchant promised to do so, and when he got home tearfully told of his misfortune. The youngest daughter, who was very understanding, immediately and without objection went to the snake's castle, although her older sisters laughed at her and mocked her

because she had not had the same wishes for jewelry and clothing. Now each time the girl sat down to eat, the snake took a seat on her lap and asked, "Will you marry me, my Darling?" But each time the girl answered, "I am afraid of you."

Now one day the girl found a mirror in which the whole world was reflected, and in it she saw her father lying in bed, sick from worry about being separated from her. She asked for a vacation, and the snake granted her a period of thirty-one days. If she stayed away one single day longer, the snake would have to die. A ring which the girl put in her mouth transported her back to the house of her father, who got well immediately when she appeared. When she told him about her life with the snake, her father advised her to answer the snake's question, saying that she would marry him. In spite of her sisters' advice to the contrary to rid herself of the snake by staying at her father's house beyond the thirty-one-day period, the girl returned on time. The snake was happy to welcome her back, and when it asked her again, "Will you marry me?" the girl answered, "Yes."

Thereupon the snake threw off its snakeskin. There before her stood a beautiful young prince, and the palace filled up with servants and people. The prince told the girl that he had been transformed into a snake as punishment for seducing an orphan and would remain so until a girl appeared who would marry him.

Now she had her father and sisters fetched. But since her sisters were green with envy and full of malice, the prince, who had learned to distinguish good from evil, transformed them into two crows. They were to remain in that form until they had cleansed themselves of their evil wishes. But the prince and his maiden celebrated their wedding and made her father the prime minister.

Now a psychological interpretation can start from the viewpoint that all the persons, actions, animals, places, and symbols appearing in the fairy tale represent intrapsychic stirrings, impulses, attitudes, modes of experience, and strivings. The fairy tale is, to a certain extent, a dream which, as Jung says, "is that theater where the dreamer is the scene, actors, prompter, director, author, public, and critic" (Jung 1981). The difference between the fairy tale and our usual night dreams is that the fairy tale contains only collective elements and has nothing to do with the richness of our personal everyday wishes, cares, and needs. Thus we find in the fairy tale only the typical, generally valid or possible forms of emotional experience.

Precisely for this reason it is also possible to interpret a fairy tale from the point of view of either masculine or feminine psychology (von Franz 1955), as well as placing it in the various stages of life. According to his or her own circumstances, the listener is free to identify with either the story's male or female main character, who then acts as does the ego in the dream. Of course there are fairy tales—and this is almost the rule—that imply an interpretation more one way or the other. In the snake fairy tale just related, the youngest daughter is the active, suffering figure who brings about the redemption of the snake. Thus it is natural to view the fairy tale as an expression of a feminine problem. But this by no means excludes the other possibility; fundamentally, the listener can also identify with the bewitched prince or with the father and interpret the fairy tale from the standpoint of masculine psychology. I will now attempt to sketch possible interpretations in their different variations.

It is not the intent of this book to illuminate and interpret an individual fairy tale in all its psychological subtleties and profundities. Whoever is looking for that is referred to the works of Hedwig von Beit (1965), Marie-Louise von Franz (1955), W. Laiblin (1960, 1961), or Aniela Jaffé (1950), to mention only a few. Here we are interested only in drawing attention to major features and connections in order to open the possibilities of understanding and to stimulate the reader to further reflection.

Surveying our fairy tale of the snake, we find something common to many fairy tales in regard to the locus of the events. There are always two worlds: the one world is that of completely natural, normal, and customary experience. In this world there lives a merchant with his two daughters, for there is no mention of a mother. He makes business trips, bringing home the little gifts still customary today. Then, quite unexpectedly, on his way home he finds himself in the other world. It is a magical world, a world in which there exists a talking snake which, moreover, even lives in a big house like a human being and has a magic mirror in which one can see the entire world. The snake can also take the daughter from one place to another effortlessly with the help of a magic ring, and in reality later turns out to be no snake at all but a bewitched prince.

If we now place these two worlds in the human soul, the first realm, in which the normal and customary take place, would correspond to consciousness. The second, the fantastic region, can be equated with the unconscious, that realm from which come dreams and fantasies in which, as is well known, everything is possible that otherwise seems impossible. Conscious and unconscious—these are the two great opposites in which the fairy tale is played out and between which it attempts to establish a relationship. The unconscious, then, can appear in many variations. Let us call to mind how many possibilities the fairy tale finds: the enchanted palace, as in this tale, or the world of Mother Holle under the earth, the journey to heaven of the "Mary's Child," the forest and the witch's house in "Hansel and Gretel," or the cave with the dragon or some other monster, the world beneath the sea, the lake, or the well.

Let us first of all try to understand the central elements of the plot in terms of the female psyche. This seems natural for this tale, since the main figure is a heroine. Here something happens that is quite similar to what happens in the well-known tale of "The Frog King" in Grimms' tales (Manheim, ed., 1983). A young girl who has lived up until now well protected in her parents' house is suddenly compelled by a seemingly chance turn of fate to accept an ugly frog, which is usually a disgusting and unpleasant—and, in the case of the snake, even very dangerous—creature, and to live with it, share her plate with it, and finally even take it to bed with her and marry it before the frog turns into a prince.

Both tales contain the motif of the loving acceptance of a cold-blooded creature. But precisely this acceptance in all its implications and this most intimate union of the ego with the unknown brings about a process of metamorphosis. A piece of healthy activity emerges from under the crust of this lowly, unpleasantly dangerous, cold-blooded animal, and an entire realm of the soul which had lain under a ban and a spell again comes to life and blossoms into active life.

The snake is an extraordinarily polyvalent symbol that occurs in mythology, in religious symbolism, and in the most varied connections and meanings in cult and rite. Its range extends from the serpent in paradise and the Midgard serpent of Germanic mythology to the Hydra and to Aesculapius' snake in Greece. Then there is Moses' brazen serpent, most worthy of reverence, or the evilly dangerous serpent heads of the Gorgon in Greek mythology. Distributed over the entire earth, this symbol occurs again and again bearing great meaning and carrying the most varied contents. Here we are obviously dealing with a piece of unconscious natural energy that is neither good nor evil, like nature itself, and that stands at the yet-undifferentiated level of the cold-blooded animals, devoid of all personal relatedness.

In the human soul it is the instinctual nature and the natural, fundamentally healthy, but as yet undifferentiated and impersonal, instinctual energy that correspond to such a piece of nature. The picture language of our tale first of all implies that this drive energy is to be identified with the sexuality arising in puberty and with the development of love relationships between man and woman. In the tale there are the following hints: first, the daughter of marriageable age, then the snake's marriage proposal. Here we also recall the quite characteristic phallic significance of the snake itself, which can become erect like the male member. At the end of the tale comes the marriage of the girl and the prince, and finally the cause for the curse on the prince, which lay in a sexual transgression.

Thus here the snake and its entire range of meaning can stand for the sexual stirrings and needs that arise in puberty in the woman's psyche. The tale shows a way of accepting and shaping what arises from the depths of her own nature and which at first appears as completely puzzling and unknown, indeed, as dangerous and disgusting. For centuries—indeed for millennia—in our culture, women have been reared in such a manner that up until marriage everything that has to do with sexuality and eroticism is supposed to be dirty and ugly and must be repressed and held down. Upon entering marriage, what previously was all bad is now suddenly supposed to become all good and all beautiful, which ultimately is just as hard to understand and just as astonishing as the transformation of a snake into a young man. Today there is clear attack under way against this prejudice, but changing or dismantling this centuries-old prejudice still lies only on the surface of consciousness for most people, while in the unconscious world of emotions it is often still quite lively and active. Just as in the tale, so, too, in reality it can then be the collective spiritual position, associated with the father archetype, which advises the girl to accept her sexuality and to live. In this, the intrapsychic father takes the place of the traditional, collective conscious attitude that prescribes what steps people are to take in certain situations. He does not even need to act as a personal father or even to be present. If this procedure succeeds, a "redemption" within the psyche really does take place, and a broad range of new experience, previously not at one's disposal, opens up.

We will not do justice to the complexity of such a dynamic collective interplay of images if we restrict such a polyvalent symbol as the snake to one meaning, that of sexuality and eroticism. Still today we tell fairy tales primarily to children, and for them, too, there must be a comprehensible meaning in the tales. Although since Freud we know that the child also is sexual and has sexual problems, its strivings for fulfillment of erotic desires is quite different from those that arise later in puberty.

If in contrast to this we think rather of the phase of defiance mentioned earlier, we can easily understand the events taking place in the tale. Similarly, the snake in the fairy tale corresponds to the psychic complex that is expressed as defiance or stubbornness. At first the girl does not fulfill the snake's wish; she refuses, and defends herself against it as a child typically fights against its aggressive impulses. Only when her father advises her to comply can the girl say yes to the snake's wish.

Also the rising affectivity and aggressivity of the phase of defiance is simultaneously good and bad. A little girl who has become stubborn and obstinate and refuses to do precisely what is wanted of her will initially get a scolding and condemnation from her parent, which classifies, for the child, too, the emerging aggressive strivings as bad. Nevertheless, her stubbornness contains something good and valuable, since it contains the first stirrings of independence and separation from the parent, a maturational step demanded also by the tradition of our culture (here again stands the father in the tale).

Today we know that the human being possesses features of both sexes not only in the body but in the psyche too; that is to say, both the man and the woman have hormones of the other sex and likewise both have masculine and feminine qualities and characteristics. Thus in psychology the active-dynamic principle is designated masculine and the passive-receptive-static principle feminine, which is not always identical with popular usage. They also appear in dreams in corresponding symbolic form. The snake and the prince in our tale correspond, in the broadest sense, to an active-dynamic natural energy that is to be redeemed from a largely unconscious and "cold-blooded" condition and made human and conscious.

A child's aggressivity toward authority figures, which arises in the phase of defiance, particularly against the mother, is initially experienced by the child itself as something foreign and not part of its own psyche. The child is, so to speak, attacked by its own aggressive stirrings. Thus it often happens that as its anger dies away, the child is the picture of stubbornness and attempts to get rid of the anger in scapegoat fashion, throwing the scapegoat, for example, in the trash can or out the window. One child I know of always threw the scapegoat in the toilet and then flushed for safety's sake. Only gradually does the child learn to master this undirected and chaotic rage and to incorporate it into the realm of psyche. From what was initially wild defiance, valuable qualities of character can develop: a degree of independence, productive activity, and self-reliance. But this can come about unhampered only if consciousness not only does not refuse, suppress, or repress these energies, but rather—to speak again in the language of our fairy-tale images—lives with them, accepts them, and ultimately is able to join with them in positive affirmation, a union that is symbolized as redemption and marriage.

If we now recognize the broader scope of the motif of the prince concealed in the animal, the way is opened to granting this process a greater degree of general validity and to understanding it in various maturational stages. This way we come closer to doing justice to the many meanings and many levels of this symbolic formulation that has arisen from the collective psyche of mankind and to the compelling power it exerts on people of various types and different ages. Fairy tales, as is well known, are not only for children. It has become less common in our rationally directed culture for adults to respond to and be interested in fairy tales, but there are many who sense in them a deeper meaning. Many of our great poets, who as artists stood especially close to influences from the unconscious, concerned themselves with fairy tales and even wrote fairy tales: Goethe, Brentano, Tieck, and E. T. A. Hoffmann, to mention only a few of those generally known. Even Shakespeare's "Midsummer Night's Dream" is a fairy tale.

To a much greater degree than with us, the fairy tale constitutes part of adult life in the orient. Up until the present time its significance corresponds approximately to what von der Leyen (1953) said of the collection, "Thousand and One Nights":

> . . . the love of and belief in these stories is something unconditional. The stories can protect him who hears them from misfortune; the condemned save or lengthen their lives with stories; stories are the greatest and purest joy of monarchs and lighten the burden of their calling; and the lowliest porter would rather forsake all earthly happiness than miss one of these tales. In an Indian fairy tale the narrator, because he interrupted his story and did not finish it, is threatened with three frightful, highly dangerous punishments by the indignant spirits who were listening. In Arabia a trip is undertaken to hear a fairy tale, and it costs more dearly than the most precious jewels. When a story is about to be told, no one steals away; even the spirits tremble with joy when they get to hear a fairy tale. Every story should be miraculous and strange, and one well-known turn of phrase says: "My story is such that, if it were engraved in the corner of your eye, it would be a warning for everyone who can be warned." Regardless how serious, how perilous, how urgent a situation may be, the

Arab will forget the rest of his life, every danger, and all his honor for a story.

Here we are talking not about children but about grown-ups. Yet today in the Orient we can meet the professional story teller. Once I myself had the opportunity to observe such a man in an out-of-the-way village in the Rif mountains. His sole requirements were an old orange crate and a stick with which he worked so convincingly that, as the occasion demanded, the crate became a house, a castle, or a cave, and the stick a prince, a princess, or a snake. Although he spoke Arabic, and we could not understand a single word, we nevertheless believed we grasped the sense of the tale. The audience, who listened rapt and fascinated to his narrative, were almost exclusively adults. He certainly could not complain of a lack of listeners, for he was always surrounded by a large circle of people.

The fairy tale was still a conscious, living part of the fantasy life of these people. In the Orient it served not only for entertainment, for some of the greatest oriental fairy-tale collections—as, for example, the Indian *Panchatantra* (Ryder, ed., 1956) or the Turkish *Parrot Book* (Hertel, trans., 1959) —were used in the rearing of young princes. According to its outer framework story (*Rahmen erzählung*), the Indian collection was expressly written for this purpose.

There we are told that in the city Mahilaropja in Dekkahn there once ruled a wise king named Amarashakti. He had three absolutely ungifted sons. Now when he saw that they had no gift for statecraft, the king called together his ministers and went into consultation with them: "Of course you know that these my sons are totally lacking in gifts. How could one contrive to awaken their reason?" Some of the ministers then said, "Majesty, the study of grammar, as we know, takes twelve years; when one has taken pains to master this, then one must study religion, statesmanship, and the art of love. All that is difficult enough for the clever; how much more so for someone of sluggish reason? For such a one the best choice is the Brahman Vishnusharman, a master of all the texts of statecraft, whose fame countless pupils proclaim." So Vishnusharman was brought to the king's court, and he declared himself ready to make the princes masters of statecraft within six months. When the king heard the Brahman's scarcely credible promise, he was just as astonished and delighted as were the ministers, and respectfully entrusted the princes to his care. Vishnusharman, however, set about instructing them in statecraft by telling them fables, and to this end he wrote five books, called the *Panchatantra*: "The Estrangement of Friends," "Winning Friends," "The War of the Crows and the

Owls," "The Loss of What Has Been Won," and "Hasty Action." Each of these five books again has its own outer story and a series of fables. The *Panchatantra* contains predominantly animal fables, and in each one there lies a useful teaching which unobtrusively plumbs the depths of a human problem. After listening to them, and after the princes had assimilated the images in the fables, the obviously neurotic impairment of their intelligence was cured.

But let us return to our tale of the snake and attempt to understand it from the standpoint of adult problems. We can then transpose it, as an inner-psychic process, to the time of midlife. This period, too, belongs among the crisis situations of human life, and many neuroses typically occur at this time. The major tasks of adaptation to outer life—such as stability in one's profession, relationships to society and to the opposite sex —should normally be resolved and mastered. One's marriage, if it has held, is now beyond the first storms. The children have long since been in school and are beginning to leave the parental home and go out into life on their own. A condition arises in which the world around one no longer offers much that is wholly new, and one's path no longer leads into life but out of it, toward the dark end, toward death.

C. G. Jung discussed this set of problems and their connection with the frequency of emotional illness in his essay, "Die Lebenswende" ["The Stages of Life"] (1969). The emotional energy which up until now has flowed into building up life is no longer demanded and becomes free. Now it actually ought to turn toward the inner world so as to deepen rather than broaden life. In point of fact, in this group of older persons we do encounter an increasing process of turning inward.

But as a rule, for one whose life up until now has been directed outward, the inner life looks just as strange and unknown as the snake appeared to the youngest daughter in the fairy tale. Often it is at just as low a developmental level as a cold-blooded creature and is totally other and totally foreign. It is just as difficult to find the right relationship to it. Thus, for example, if we again look at the fairy tale from the feminine viewpoint, a woman, who up until now has lived entirely for her children, will have to seek new tasks when her children no longer need her. If she is clever and if she does not cling to her children beyond the appropriate time as the burdensome mother-in-law, the woman may then turn to long-neglected spiritual and intellectual possibilities which up until now have lain undeveloped in her. In developing this new side in herself she can discover an "inner prince" and revivify a realm in need of redemption.

In contrast to the feminine materia, the spiritual-intellectual forces contained in her own inner nature are, as a rule, characterized in psychology as masculine, as I explained earlier. For a person of strong emotions they are often unpleasant, indeed even distasteful, when one becomes aware of them, so that accepting and loving them becomes a difficult task. Thus here the prince would correspond to such an innate masculine principle in the woman, a principle the development of which would bring the woman to a deepened capacity for judgment in her views on the world and on life. It leads to the "formation of one's own spiritual stance which delivers one from the limitations and entrapment of the narrowly personal" (E. Jung 1981) and can be available to consciousness as an actively creative force. I believe that this problem plays an important role in the present day. To a great extent, woman's restriction to house and kitchen has been abolished, the average life expectancy has been considerably lengthened, and the extended family in which the woman beyond the midpoint in life could somehow still find in the so-called "feminine framework" her realm of activity, no longer exists. And her own children, too, usually no longer marry and live in the same or in the nearby village but often move away, sometimes to the other side of the continent. There is nothing left for the woman in midlife but to accept the loneliness and the feeling of being left behind and to seek in herself the balance and a new fulfillment. I have treated this group of problems extensively in my book on midlife (1968b).

As already mentioned, it is more natural to interpret this snake fairy tale from the viewpoint of feminine psychology. Later I will cite a similar tale, "The Three Feathers," in which the interpretation from the masculine side is more natural. But it was said earlier that it is possible to analyze a fairy tale from both masculine and feminine standpoints. All these figures in the tale—including the hero or the heroine—are, basically, not the human ego but archetypal figures. As Max Luethi (1947) says, the fairy-tale heroes or heroines are "pure carriers of action," lacking profundity and the world of human feelings. Hence the hero is, on the one hand, superhuman insofar as he is able to accomplish deeds which human ego by itself could not have done; but on the other hand, he stands lower than the human level as a consequence of his distinct one-sidedness and lack of variability and depth.

Hence it is more correct to conceptualize the hero or the heroine as a functional complex which, in the appropriate and corresponding situation, to be sure, permits of a temporary identification but never of a lasting one. If, for example, a child falls from a bridge into the water, and without thinking a young man jumps in after and saves the child, his ego identified meaningfully for a short time with the hero archetype. But if someone continually tries to play the hero and disregards the necessary safety measures and the vitally important measure of fear and cowardice, then it is a case of "fabulous" stupidity which often enough places life under a death penalty. Later in the course of this book we will describe what unadapted and morbid features appear when a person confuses himself or his conscious ego with such an archetypal image as the fairy-tale figure represents, and to what a great degree disturbed persons often do that.

The individual figures of the fairy tale, including the hero or the heroine, represent the possibilities of emotional experience, and, given this assumption, the central figure of our fairy tale, the youngest daughter, can stand for the man's emotional side. In this fashion the entire tale can then be interpreted also from the standpoint of the man's psyche. As the starting point here I again take the midlife situation just described, in which a new and revised orientation should come about in the natural course of the process of human maturation. The course of the tale, that is, the translation of the story line into psychological reality, would then be understood as follows.

Such a man might have spent his life up until now developing primarily his thinking function. The new orientation of midlife would now demand that precisely the opposite to this be developed, i.e., that his active interest turn more toward the inner world and toward the deepening—rather than the broadening—of experience by way of which the development of feeling takes its course. But the demands that this youngest and least undeveloped side makes—corresponding to the daughter's wish for roses that just at this time have ripened and are plentiful and inexpensive in the markets—are not so easy to fulfill as it appears at first. Their fulfillment is at the mercy of all sorts of chance occurrences and disagreements which ultimately lead to a confrontation with the magical-mythological realm of images in one's own inner world. But it is precisely to these images that one must pay emotional attention and active interest (this corresponds in the fairy tale to delivering the daughter to the snake); in doing this, a temporarily severe crisis situation arises (the father's illness in the tale).

Everybody knows crises of this sort and the ebb of psychic energy into the unconscious where all feelings and thoughts appear to circle sterilely about the same problem, and there is no more attention left for the world around one. Only by recognizing the situation and by casting a bridge between the two realms—the conscious and the unconscious (here the fairy tale utilizes the motif of the mirror and the daughter's partial return to her parent's home)—does the desperately stuck condition begin to break up. Due to the bond and obligation to the unconscious realm (the promise of return in the fairy tale), a simple restitution of the previous condition is no longer possible. One must not heed the voices (personified in the tale by the two sisters) which whisper: "Forget the whole thing. Remain as you were. After all, you had great success that way. You don't need to subject yourself to the laborious process of maturation and change." These are negative, tenacious, unproductive anxieties. Only through a renewed and this time voluntary turn toward the inner world (corresponding to the daughter's return) and a loving acceptance of it (as is symbolized by the marriage) do the values lying in own's own inner nature become accessible. This leads to a broadening of consciousness and to an enlargement of the personality (as seen in the redeemed land and the return of the prince and the princess from the magical realm). To a certain extent, the individual now has at his disposal two realms: the realm of the outer and that of the inner world. The fairy-tale prince delivered from the snake then represents the highest values contained in one's own inner nature, values freed from an unconscious condition, thanks to conscious effort.

In many fairy tales this figure then assumes the highest place in the psyche and relieves the old king or father, as is suggested here, too. This would correspond to a reorientation of the scale of values as again and again happens in the healthy process of life. What in our youth appeared as the greatest and most important thing can, for the mature individual, no longer be of such great significance. New, different values replace the old. If the largely biological tasks of the first half of life—for a man the founding of a family and the securing of his existence—are fulfilled, then in their place one's interest should gradually turn toward social and cultural tasks. Then there takes shape within a new value (a young king who takes over the government) which the ego has to serve.

This process of personality development, in which life no longer is oriented toward its biological goals, is equally true for men and women. Here the task is posed of developing what is specifically human, even if it may prove necessary to go against nature. Again and again somewhere in ourselves we run up against the snake, our own drive nature, and in a laborious and painful process we must free it from its pure brutishness, a process which always remains incomplete and much too often miscarries or does not even take place.

Clinical Parallel

As we have seen, this so extraordinarily common and many-layered redemption motif may be filled with a different content in various phases of
life. Now we might say that all these are perhaps clever and interesting interpretations, but that they remain speculative, and their relevance for human beings is highly questionable. Consequently I would like to share the
dream of a twenty-four-year-old woman which clearly parallels this fairy
tale. Even if the characteristics of the individual actions are of course
different, in both the motif of the transformation of the snake into a prince
still holds center stage. Here I must add that just as the interpretation of
dream symbols figures in a course of treatment, so, too, the interpretation of fairy-tale dreams is determined by the patient's spontaneous associations. As I have already discussed, the symbol of the snake, and hence
all other symbols, can have many meanings. That content which arises
through the patient's associations and situation in life is to be included in
the interpretation. Now the dream of my patient.

> I was with my boyfriend in a circus tent. There was another, full-
> bosomed girl who was after my boyfriend and who resembled
> me. She also brought another young man with her whom my
> boyfriend, who was now the circus manager, was supposed to
> employ. I was not interested in him. Then in the evening I went
> through the fence of the circus area across a street to the woods. A
> snake with golden spots on its body was wound around a tree.
> This snake was the young man from earlier, and I thought, "You
> don't need to be afraid." Then suddenly a wolf attacked me, and
> then the snake changed back into the young man who defended
> me against the wolf.

Precisely as in the fairy tale, in this dream we have the two different worlds,
the everyday world of reality depicted in the events of the circus, and the
other, magical world, which begins beyond the fence.

Her boyfriend was more than twenty years her senior, hence a sort of
father figure, and, as in the fairy tale, here, too, there is a conflictual tension
between the patient and a female figure of the same age. In the fairy tale
this tension is portrayed in the relationship of the heroine to her two sisters.
The patient had a distinct fear of snakes, and in earlier dreams they had always been most threatening. So here the emphasis, "You don't need to be

afraid," indicates a change in the emotional attitude experienced toward the animal, similar to the change in the fairy tale. Following this change in attitude in the dream there also takes place the re-transformation of the snake into a human being.

This young woman was suffering from a severe neurosis which had made her practically incapable of work since the age of sixteen. There had been a severe disturbance and paralysis of activity so that she could not finish school and had acquired no training for any future job. Hence she remained dependent on other people and had an excessive need to be taken care of.

After she had been in treatment for some time, she brought this dream. It had greatly impressed her, but at first she could not make any sense of it. During this period of her analysis after we had reduced the intensity of a number of anxieties, the problem of again finding her lost productive activity and looking for her own job became acute. In fact, a short time after this dream, the patient did undertake job training which she pursued and successfully completed. Thus the prince symbolized for her a piece of productive activity which in changed form and freed of false fears is in a position to vanquish the destructive-devouring wolf. We know this kind of wolf from the story of "Little Red Riding Hood." There he appears in place of the good grandmother and thus represents a negative-demonic aspect of the feminine and of the mother-child relationship. This patient's associations to the wolf, too, pointed to a feminine-maternal symbol. In terms of her problem it would then have to do with her infantile dependency on a maternal-nurturing person and with her inability to live alone and independently.

In contrast with the fairy tale, here the simple, loving acceptance of the previously feared personality component is not sufficient to bring about liberation, redemption, and healing of the psyche, but rather in addition the threatening wolf appears, too. Yet another conflict with a negative tendency which threatens to destroy the patient must be settled. Just as in life it is not always enough simply to unite lovingly with something so that it enters the personality as one's own possession but one must make efforts and suffer difficulties to achieve it, so in the fairy tale exactly this complex of problems appears. Two of the previously mentioned variations on our snake tale show additional sides of this problem.

German Version

In the German tale, "The Snake," a countess gives birth to a snake as punishment for her quarrelsome marriage. One day the snake demands from its mother a woman it can marry. The countess now persuades a poor girl who tends the chickens in the yard to marry the snake. As the poor girl is praying before an image of Mary, the image suddenly begins to speak and gives the girl some advice: on the wedding night when the snake says "Take off your clothes," the girl should demand seven times that the snake itself undress first. The snake would then shed its skin seven times and on the seventh time a handsome prince would stand before her. The girl follows the advice, and when the next morning the countess comes to the door of the bride chamber, her son, freed from the spell, and the girl approach her. At first their joy is great, but with time the mother regrets seeing her son married to a girl of such lowly origins, and she keeps dinning it into his ears to reject the girl. But he remains steadfast and rejects the incessant demands of his mother until she finally gives up her evil intentions.

We see how in this variation the accent rests much more emphatically on the transformation motif of shedding the skin, which the girl must make happen seven times. The number seven is a magical and sacred number in myths, fairy tales, and in folk belief. This repeated molting itself indicates a significantly increased expenditure of energy directed toward the unconscious content. Moreover, the unconscious content must be repeatedly defended against the mother's negative influence. The obviously quarrelsome and envious countess corresponds, then, at another level to the wolf in the patient's dream.

Albanian Version

Things do not always turn out so smoothly and so well as in this variation. In the Albanian tale, "The Snake Child," the redemption is at first lost again. Here a queen makes a pact with her friend, the wife of the vizier, who has three daughters, that her (the queen's) still-unborn son shall marry one of these three daughters. She then gives birth to a snake, and when it is grown, she demands that the mother of the girls fulfill the agreement. Twice the vizier's wife rejects the queen when she asks the two older daughters. Finally the snake threatens to come at night and kill all three if he is not given the third and youngest as wife.

The youngest daughter now goes to an old wise woman who advises her to put on forty petticoats, one over the other. Here, too, on the wedding night whenever the snake demands that she get undressed, she should demand the same from the snake and each time take off only one petticoat. After the fortieth molting, a beautiful prince would stand before her. And so it happens, but the prince now demands of the girl that she keep all this silent until the birth of their child. In the morning, he slips back into a snake skin, transforming himself back into a prince again only for their evenings together. For eight months the girl withstands all her mother's questions about the marriage with the snake until she finally bursts forth with the truth. Now the snake locks her out of the castle and vanishes.

The unhappy girl goes into the world in search of her prince. Again she encounters an old wise woman who advises her to climb a distant mountain. There she would find dirty water with lots of worms. If she drinks a mouthful of it, the earth will open before her. Below she would then meet the two daughters of the sun who could tell her where her husband was to be found.

The girl follows this advice and the older daughter of the sun shows her the house in the underworld where her husband lives with another woman. At the same time she gives her a walnut, a hazelnut, and an almond. The girl now takes lodging as a nun in her husband's house, and first opens the walnut, out of which falls a golden hen with chicks. Since the other woman wants them, the wife disguised as a nun demands a night with her husband as the price for them. The woman agrees, but drugs him with a sleeping potion. The next day the girl opens the hazelnut, which contains a golden parrot. The same thing happens again, but this time during the night a coppersmith has heard the heard the laments of the girl who again and again called, "Give me the silver key so that I can give birth to the golden child!" The coppersmith tells this to the snake prince, who greatly marvels at it. The next day the girl opens the almond, which contains a golden cradle. Again the woman wants this precious treasure and is ready to give up her husband for a night in order to get it. But this time, however, the prince pours out the sleeping potion. Now he recognizes his first wife and flees back to the upper world with her.

Here the fairy tale symbolizes that a value already won can again be lost if there is not adequate stability. In life, too, we often have the experience of believing we have already accomplished a developmental step. It is at that precise moment that one easily gets inattentive and careless and again loses what has almost been gained. Thus the girl must undertake the laborious pilgrimage into the magical realm of the unconscious, where the reunion succeeds on the third try. These three attempts are identical with the extremely common three tests through which the hero or the heroine must pass. A detailed interpretation of this symbolism is found in Erich Neumann's study of the "Amor and Psyche" fairy tale (1973a).

We want to take a look at the "heroines" of these three variations of the fairy tale, since in them a very typical and frequent fairy-tale figure occurs. In the Greek and the Albanian versions, it is the youngest daughter, and in the German version the poor girl who tends the chickens. The fairy tales uncommonly often make use of this motif in which always the youngest, least adroit, and seemingly weakest must traverse the heroic path. That is true not only for the female figure here, but, to mention only two examples, also for the male central figure in "The Three Feathers" of the Grimm Brothers and in the Russian tale "The Maiden Czar."

Viewed psychologically, this inferior, despised, and unadapted figure corresponds to a function of psyche not yet developed. Of the abundance of developmental possibilities from which individuals can form their personalities, as a rule it is first the inherently best and those most suited for the given environment who are developed and cultivated. Thus, for example, a person well endowed with intellect who, moreover, lives in a rationally oriented world will first school, cultivate, and develop the intellect. That person is also in a position to solve a great part of the life problems encountered by using trained thinking. Other functions, on the other hand, will remain undifferentiated and archaic; indeed, the moreso to the extent that they are suited to disturbing the leading function. As is well known, feeling opposes thinking. Thinking makes its decisions according to the principle of "true and untrue" or "right and wrong," whereas feeling judges according to "congenial or not congenial." But precisely what is right and true can be uncongenial according to feeling, and vice versa, hence the person who thinks exactly excludes the influences of feeling as often as possible. That does not mean that such a person has no feelings, but just as in the body an untrained and unused muscle remains weak and inferior or even degenerates, so, too, in the emotional realm feeling remains undifferentiated, unadapted, and inferior in a person predominantly oriented by thinking.

Now at the beginning of our fairy tale there is the very common group of four: the father and the three daughters (in other tales also a father with three sons or a mother with three daughters), which intrapsychically correspond to the four basic psychic functions—thinking, feeling, sensing, and intuiting—described by C. G. Jung (1913). The heroine is the youngest, that is, the one that appeared last and is the weakest. In the German variant of our tale it is the "chicken girl," that is, the inferior and despised one. If we follow the example mentioned above, then the father or the mother would correspond to the fully developed leading function—thinking; the two sisters to the developed auxiliary functions of sensing and intuiting, which do not need significantly to disturb thinking; while the youngest daughter corresponds to the undifferentiated function of feeling. Her wish for a bouquet of roses, a typical symbol of feeling, would then also fit well with this conception. Precisely this inferior and neglected function is in the position to solve the problems which have arisen in this psyche and to free the new value from the unconscious. In life this would correspond to a situation in which we cannot go further with our customary and habitual ways, attitudes, and behaviors, and must reach back for something very unaccustomed and unpracticed. We are compelled to solve a problem with precisely our weakest side, which, for example, can then occur if a "thinker" falls in love or if at midlife the further course of life demands of us new behaviors, attitudes, and forms of experiencing.

The Tale of the Three Feathers

In the tale of "The Three Feathers," this set of problems appears yet more clearly than in the snake fairy tales discussed above (Manheim, 1983). A king has three sons, of whom two are considered clever, but the third is called Blockhead. When the king gets old and weak, he cannot decide which son should inherit his kingdom. So he tells them he will decide the succession on the basis of who brings him the finest carpet. He casts three feathers into the air and commands his sons to "go as they fly." The one feather flies east, the other west, but the third straight ahead and falls to the earth. The two older brothers, who go east and west, laugh at Blockhead, who must stay where the feather has fallen. He sits down sadly, but beside the feather he suddenly notices a trap-door, which he raises and under which he finds a stairs. He descends, comes to another door, and knocks. Thereupon from the other side of the door a voice calls out:

> Little green maid
> Perched on a log,

Hobgoblin's dog,
Wobblin' goblin,
Quick, go and see
What that knocking can be.

The door opens, and the king's son sees a big fat toad sitting there surrounded by many small toads. When he presents his request, the toad has a large box brought and from it she gives Blockhead a carpet, "so fine that nothing like it could have been woven on the earth above."

Since they had no faith in their youngest brother, the two older brothers have taken no pains at all and brought coarse cloth from a shepherdess. Since the king must decide in favor of the youngest who produced the finest carpet and won the contest, the two older brothers demand a new test. The father demands the most beautiful ring and again throws three feathers in the air. His feather again leads the youngest to the trap-door, and from the toad he receives a ring, "which was set with glittering gems and was so beautiful that no goldsmith on earth could have made it."

The haughty older brothers bring the rim of an old cartwheel. Again the father grants the realm to the youngest. But at his older sons' insistence he sets yet one more condition: that of finding the most beautiful wife. The toad gives Blockhead a hollowed-out carrot with six mice harnessed to it. She commands the disappointed king's son to set one of the little toads in the carrot carriage. He randomly picks one from the circle. As it sits down in the carriage, suddenly it turns into the the most beautiful maiden, the carrot changes into a coach, and the six mice become horses. He kisses her and with her races to the king, to whom his brothers have brought mere peasant women.

Again, the king awards his kingdom to the youngest, only to be challenged anew by the older brothers who demand that their father set yet a fourth test. The women will have to jump through a hoop. The two older brothers believe that the strong peasant women can do this more readily than the delicate maiden. But the peasant women were so clumsy that each broke arms and legs, while the beautiful maiden "glided through the ring as lightly and easily as a deer." And so the crown went to Blockhead and he reigned wisely for many years. (A fuller interpretation of this fairy tale can be found in H. von Beit [1960, vol. 1, pp. 337ff], which I have given here in abbreviated form.)

Basically we are dealing here with the same motif as in the first tale: redeeming something from its captivity in a cold-blooded animal form and letting it become human. Here the toad has taken the place of the snake symbol. The tale expressly emphasizes that it is a question not only of the youngest, but also of the dumbest, son, that is, the unadapted and inferior part of the personality which here becomes the real hero. The two better trained and adapted brothers actually fail the tests miserably, and in place of genuine values they attain something only mediocre: in place of a carpet, coarse cloth; in place of a ring, a cartwheel rim; and in place of a fine young lady, rough peasant girls. Here is expressed the fact that in a special situation that doesn't occur every day, the trained functions are in a position to achieve only the commonplace and the usual, what has been known and possible for a long time, whereas the truly valuable and unusual can be reached only by unusual means, even if we are bungling and clumsy, as we always are when our usual weapons fail.

Now one could assume that this type of fairy tale about a king and his three sons is particularly informative for problems of psychological type. Unfortunately, this assumption is deceptive, and it is an extraordinarily difficult and complex undertaking to relate fairy tales and psychological functions. As a rule it remains open as to which of the four functions is to be assigned to the hero. The same holds true for attitude type, since one seldom can speak of a purely introverted or extraverted hero; rather the hero has to experience both introverted and extraverted phases in the course of his quest. In the tale of the three feathers the youngest son must remain at the spot and go down into the ground while his brothers can ride east and west seeking to fulfill the task. Hence we would say that he introverts, or turns inward. But on the other hand he extraverts, or turns outward, again to the extent that, in the confrontation with his two brothers in which he succeeds, he outwardly displays the treasures received from the toad: the carpet, the ring, and the anima. Neither his behavior nor the symbolism gives any information on his function type. One could assume that as Blockhead he has inferior thinking, and in point of fact nothing is said about him regarding thinking; he sits sadly beside his feather (feeling) that has fallen to the ground. He sees the door that leads into the earth to the cave of the toad (sensation). And, finally, he calls on intuition with the possibility of transforming a homely carrot into an elegant carriage with a princess. Indeed, his two brothers think that Blockhead can accomplish nothing significant, so they take no pains in their search for the values. But their thinking is clearly inferior, as they do not even smart after their first defeats. Thus one is inclined to ascribe better thinking to Blockhead even if it is not expressly mentioned. In my opinion it remains totally open as to which function in the tale is supposed to be carried into consciousness by the hero, and the fairy tale actually documents only the fundamental question of the development of an inferior function.

It is not, however, an unequivocal rule that no specific function is assigned to the hero; rather, there are tales in which that happens incomprehensibly. In the oriental fairy-tale cycle, "The Story of the Porter and the Three Ladies," which I interpreted elsewhere in detail (Dieckmann, 1974), the hero of the tale of the second blind beggar is clearly a thinking type. As I discussed, he still has to confront the development of his auxiliary sensation function with his undifferentiated feeling function, which brings his downfall when he attempts to integrate it. Hence even in reference to the problem of differentiating psychological type, the fairy tale leaves it open, which, however, from the standpoint of an individual who selects a certain tale, can be answered in some cases, a topic I will return to in Chapter 5 on the favorite fairy tale from childhood. I have treated this issue in detail in another work (Dieckmann, 1975).

Citing one example, the tale of the snake, I have been concerned in this chapter to give a glimpse of the breadth of possible points of view from which one can understand the images and symbols of these stories. For some readers this approach may be too multivocal, and they will incline to hold only *one* interpretation as correct and see in a tale a more narrowly defined, individual problem. Such a view, in my opinion, does not recognize that the fairy tale is capable of arousing lively interest at practically every stage of life and at every level of maturation—an interest that far exceeds the tale's purely aesthetic value, which, moreover, can often be quite meager. Hence the fairy tale must again and again say something to the person receptive to it; it must touch something in the depths and set it in motion, something which cannot be better or otherwise expressed and formulated than in these images.

The ever-recurring symbolism, too, has remained the same in its major features across the centuries and millennia during the development of our culture. Already in the oldest fairy tale we know, the Egyptian brother tale from the nineteenth dynasty (ca. 1220 B.C. (Brunner-Traut, ed. and trans., 1963), we encounter the motif of transformation and re-transformation of man into animal and plant, the motif of the meeting between humans and gods, the motif of enchantment and of talking animals. It does not differ essentially in its basic features from the tales we still tell today.

The fundamental problems of human existence last not only through our whole personal life but through the life of humanity. Each age must understand, formulate, and interpret them, just as we must do at each stage of our life. Thus our possibilities of understanding circle around the primordial image, and at every new level another facet of the inherent meaning shines forth. We will never understand them fully, and thus there remains a bit of mystery that always and again attracts us and challenges us to reflect. Even without any conscious interpretation, the fairy tale speaks to us, and to everyone it addresses the currently acute problem. Thus it exercises its effect also beneath the knowing consciousness. Consciousness only deepens or strengthens it.

CHAPTER 3

Are Fairy Tales Only for Children?

Knowing, rational consciousness arises only in the course of the process of development and maturation. According to the results of psychoanalytic investigations, it begins to form about the sixth year of life. Up until then the child lives in a magical-mythological world in which, along with a dark awareness of drives and instincts, an imagistic consciousness first arises in which magical and mythological motifs, images, identifications, reactions, attitudes, behaviors, and practices exist side by side. This level in the early development of consciousness and of a world view which, according to Cassirer (1953–57), thinks complexly and contains the identity of the fundamental gestalt, is the earliest origin of the spirit. This graphic mythological experiencing of the world always remains as a foundation beneath our rational thought processes and has a by no means only regressive-negative character that finds expression in superstition and neuroses. On the contrary, this layer of emotionally, highly charged images and fantasies is also the foundation for new emotional acquisitions as well as for the processes of change and maturation in the psyche of adults. Even in the realm of scientific research the importance of such archetypal images has been confirmed, and the physicist Pauli (1952) has pointed out that in

> the development of scientific ideas every act of understanding is a wearisome process ushered in by unconscious processes long before the content of consciousness can be formulated rationally. As organizers and shapers in this world of symbolic images, the archetypes function as the necessary bridge between the sense perceptions and ideas, and are ac-

cordingly also a necessary prerequisite if ideas in natural science are to
arise.

In the light of these reflections the question of telling fairy tales to children and of stimulating them to deal with this magical-mythological level
and of moving in it takes on a color that is usually overlooked or paid little
attention. Our age, too, often discusses the question of whether it makes
sense to tell children fairy tales. Some reject them as outmoded, magical,
or antiquated, or reproach them for the cruelty present in them. Yet others
cling to them piously, romantically, or often with sentimental memories of
their own and actively defend them. But, untouched by such discussions,
fairy tales continue to be told; children hungrily snatch them up, usually
leaving their fanciest technological toys lying there if they can hear a fairy
tale, and fairy tales again assume their old value and significance in the
lives of children, regardless of all the talk.

The issue of being "for" or "against" the fairy tale, moreover, is very old
and was formulated almost a hundred years ago by the poet Wilhelm Hauff
(1896). Hauff prefaced his fairy-tale collection with a story which he called
"The Fairy Tale as Almanac." At that time the significance of the almanac
approximated that of the popular scientific book of today. Now in this
story, Hauff describes how Poor Fairy Tale is driven out by rationally en-
lightened people and flees crying to its mother, Fantasy. Mother Fantasy is
most indignant that the sentries set up by humans before her world no
longer want to let her oldest and dearest daughter come in. She justifiably
suspects that evil, old Auntie Fashion has slandered Fairy Tale. Inventive
as she is, she disguises Fairy Tale by tailoring an almanac for her garment,
and so attired sends her back to human beings. Unfortunately the sentries
spot that Fairy Tale is hiding in this dress and laugh at her, but Fairy Tale
leads them up the garden path with the colorful images of her stories until
they fall asleep. A friendly man then takes Fairy Tale by the hand and leads
her past the sleeping sentries to the children.

It seems appropriate to concern ourselves with the question of the fairy
tale from the viewpoint of psychology and to set aside the aesthetic and
moral viewpoints around which conflict usually breaks out. What does a
fairy tale really mean for the soul of the child? What significance can it have
above and beyond mere pleasure and entertainment? How does such a
strong interest arise for such an artistically meager creation? These are all
questions that confront us if we want to concern ourselves with this phenomenon.

In order to arrive at a meaningful answer, it is necessary to think somewhat differently from the way we are otherwise accustomed to do in our
cultural area. As a rule, our concepts and thoughts orient us toward the
outer world and from it we derive our standards of judgment. But if we apply these to the fairy tale, it turns into hair-raising nonsense which we
should not under any circumstances pass on to credulous children. Due to
atmospheric conditions alone you cannot possibly build a gingerbread
house in the forest, and who among us would, for example, marry a princess on a pea who bruises at every handshake or kiss?

The view is often expressed that in the case of the creations of fantasy
which appear in myth and fairy tale, we are dealing with memory traces of
a long past age in the development of humanity. Hence the dragon would
be a memory of the saurians of primeval times; the giant bird Roch of the
Arabic tales would resemble the original bird, the archaeopteryx; and the
like. Certainly there may be a trace of truth in this; we need think, say, of
the flood and the evidence of natural events and catastrophies that actually
have afflicted humanity in prehistoric times. The scientific search for these
connections between the mythologem and the events that actually tran-
spired in the outer world stands today in full flower. The success of such a
work as *Und die Bibel hat doch Recht* (Keller, 1955) speaks for itself. But
in many places this line of inquiry probably goes too far. I cite the very
witty parody entitled, *The Truth About Hansel and Gretel* (Traxler,
1963). In this book, the author proves with scientific scrupulosity, precisely
in the style of the usual publications in this field, that the fairy tale of Hansel
and Gretel arose out of an actual situation, namely the conflict between
two parties in the Middle Ages, both interested in a recipe for gingerbread.

Up to a certain point the establishment of relationships between fairy
tale, myth, saga, legend, etc., and the environment may certainly be
justified. But in life humankind stands opposite not only the great tasks of
experiencing, enduring, mastering, and shaping the environment but must
simultaneously fulfill a second task of at least equal magnitude which lies in
the mastery and formation of our own inner worlds. The inner world as mi-
crocosm stands opposite the outer as macrocosm and without doubt is just
as significant and extensive. If we proceed from the idea that the fairy tale,
just as the myth or, at the highest level, religion, is to be understood as a
part of this inner world and as a means for shaping it, we can gain an insight into the meaning and essence of the fairy tale, which gives answers to
many questions. Here, after all, in the inner world all these strange and
marvelous things that appear in fairy tales really do exist. We do not at all

need to go back to distant ages to find, say, a dragon; it lives in the unconscious today, here and now, as, for example, in the following dream of a
twenty-five-year-old male patient.

> I am in a house which is shaped like a half sphere. A dragon
> comes and devours all the people. He wants to get into the house.
> Old weapons are lying about, and when the dragon tries to get in
> a window, I throw axes at him. He falls over like a rubber doll, but
> straightens up again. With pistols and knives I battle the dragon,
> who has now forced his way into the room. He wants to swallow
> me, but now I try to bargain with him. But suddenly he has gulped
> me down. But I am still alive and I say to him that he must throw
> up, and then he would be rid of me again. The dragon retches
> and retches but he has no feeling of nausea.

The young man had a severe neurosis, and his major problem at this
time was that of asserting himself against the demands and eruptions of
dark drives, e.g., to destroy or smash something valuable. This dark, destructive drive energy dwelling in him appears in the image of the dragon,
and in the dream he experiences the ancient fairy tale and myth motif of
the battle with the dragon. We see also that he has little success here and
his still weak ego cannot withstand the drive need and is overcome.

I would like to use this dream, however, only as an example for the living existence of fairy tale motifs in the unconscious, as an indication of its
significance for coming to terms with inner forces, and not discuss it in detail. Rather, I would like to return to the fairy tale itself and stimulate the
reader to reflect on the significance of the fairy tale for the child.

As a rule, the fairy tale is the first and earliest mentally formed cultural
product with which the human being comes in contact and assimilates. Ex-
cepting fairy tales by known authors, it originates not in the fantasy world
of an individual person but rather belongs to the collective intellectual creations of a cultural area on which probably an infinite number of people
have also worked before it was set in the written form known to us. In
other cultures and in earlier times, as already mentioned, the fairy tale has
very often been considered of great value in the education and intellectual
formation of the individual. It has even been used for healing. In Hindu
medicine there is a method of cure for emotionally disoriented persons: a
fairy tale depicting their problems is read to them, and they are supposed
to meditate on it (Chaplin, 1930). All these conceptions proceed from the
idea that there is more contained in the fairy tale than only a pretty and in-

teresting story. They are based on the supposition that the fairy tale has value and, under certain conditions, curative value in forming and shaping the human inner world. The figures and forms, as well as the plot, of the fairy tale are, then, in this view, no longer experienced as an empirically existing series of events taking place in the outer world but rather as personifications of inner psychic structures and developments. They are symbols and represent something that runs its course in humankind's emotional dynamics for which no more apt and no better image could be found. (I draw here on the concept of the symbol as defined by C. G. Jung in *Psychological Types*, [1913]). In the remainder of this chapter I will consider one of the best-known German fairy tales, "Hansel and Gretel," from this viewpoint, and will discuss it in the light of a specific problem in the emotional development of a child. Briefly I will sketch the content in its usual version found in the Grimm Brothers' collection (Manheim, 1983).

"Hansel and Gretel"

The fairy tale takes us to a woodcutter's family in which dire need reigns. There is not even enough bread to go around, and so the parents decide, on the stepmother's initiative, to abandon both children to the forest. But the children hear of this plan, and Hansel collects pebbles which he drops all along the path so that they can find their way back. When they have arrived in the forest, the parents light a fire, give the children the last piece of bread, and tell them to lie down while their father cuts wood nearby. Then they deceived the children by letting them think that a dead branch beating in the wind against the tree trunk was really their father's axe, and secretly they went home. Hansel and Gretel, who had fallen asleep by the fire, waited until nightfall and found their way back home with the help of the pebbles.

But it is not long before the same situation faces the family again, and this time the stepmother locks the door so that no pebbles can be collected. Consequently, Hansel uses bread crumbs to mark the path. This time both children are again abandoned in the forest and left on their own.

After they have wandered about for three days, they encounter a beautiful snow-white bird that sings marvelously. They follow it and it leads them to a little house "made of bread, and the roof . . . made of cake and the windows of sparkling sugar." The well-known scene ensues in which the children eat of the house; and when the witch (who lives inside) asks who is nibbling on her house, they answer, "The wind so wild,/The heavenly child." Then the witch takes the children in, feeds them lavishly, and gives them a soft bed. "Actually she was a wicked witch . . . [who] killed, cooked, and ate any child who fell into her hands." And so the next morning she locks Hansel in a little shed to fatten him like a goose, having a plan to later eat him and his sister. She forces Gretel to cook and clean for her.

Thanks only to Hansel's trick (holding out a little bone rather than his finger for the witch to test how fat he is getting) can the fate of being eaten be initially stayed. Finally, however, Gretel must heat the oven, ostensibly to bake bread but actually to roast the children. Gretel realizes this and she tricks the witch ("How do I get in?") to climb into the oven, and the witch burns up. The children are freed; they load up all the treasures the witch had hoarded and set out homeward.

Now, on the way home, they come to a great body of water they cannot cross, which bounds the magical realm, the witch's forest. Here Gretel sees a white duck, and asks for its help in crossing the water. Hansel wants them both to cross together, but Gretel insists they go separately, and so it carries first Gretel and then Hansel across the water. When they get home, the stepmother is dead and the father and the children can now live "in pure happiness" and without difficulty on the booty taken from the witch.

It will be to our advantage in our reflections to begin with the central figure of the plot, the witch. Two characteristics of this witch stand out. For one, she is obviously evil through and through, in contrast to other, similar fairy-tale figures, such as Mother Holle in "The Widow's Two Daughters," who shows her evil, witchy aspect only toward the lazy girl. Secondly, she very clearly and visibly has something to do with food: she is the resident of an edible cottage. It is stressed that she lavishly feeds the half-starved children who appear at her door. Then she fattens Hansel, and finally she has in mind to boil, roast, and eat the children. Thus in the person of this witch one of the immensely deep, early, and archaic problems of humankind appears to be embodied, of which the German poet Schiller (n.d.) wrote:

> Meanwhile, until Philosophy
> Holds the world together,
> She (nature) sustains the bustle
> Through hunger and through love.

This witch is an evil, demonic mother figure who uses the children's hunger to entice them into her power, to hold them captive, to exploit their

labor—as in the instance of Gretel—for highly egotistic ends, and ultimately to devour them. First of all we can ask: Are there mothers like this?
To this question we must answer with both yes and no; with no because in
a human being pure evil probably never or only very rarely occurs, and
with yes because very many mothers unfortunately possess this more-or-
less unconscious trait of holding on to their child by spoiling it, buying its
love with candy, hindering its growth toward independence, and exploiting
its life for the satisfaction of their own needs and demands.

Fairy-tale figures are types, and they embody only typical, generally human characteristics but often lack the conflicting or concurrent multiplicity
of emotional currents and properties which constitute a real person. M.
Luethi (1947), in particular, has drawn attention to this. We know many
instances of severe childhood neuroses in which a "devouring mother
love" actually has swallowed the developing child's own personality. If we
are honest with ourselves, even we will discover, to a greater or lesser extent, such traits in ourselves.

Again and again we must submit ourselves to serious self-education in
order to prevent us from using our children to satisfy our own demands.

These reflections, which I do not want to pursue further, give us *one* answer to the question of the psychological significance of the fairy tale for
the child: From fairy-tale figures the child experiences and learns to deal
with the demands and needs impinging on it from figures in its own environment, demands and needs dangerous to its own personality. It experiences how one can endure vis-à-vis overwhelming powers, such as adults
are when compared with the child. It learns what forms and possibilities
there are of dealing with these powers and ultimately how one can overcome them.

But I believe that this side is not the most important; consequently we
now want to take a further step, which I have already mentioned, by trans-
posing the fairy tale and its cast into the child's inner world. In the witch we
would no longer see the negative side of an "overprotective mother,"
which actually exists in the environment, but rather we would see that this
figure embodies a problem within the child. Thus we assume, to put it
quite simply, that there exists something in the child itself that we can des-
ignate as witch. Now in order to answer what it is we are dealing with, we
first must turn back to our fairy tale.

The tale of Hansel and Gretel again shows a clear division into two
different worlds. First there is the empirical, everyday world in which a simple woodcutter and his family live, and then in the mysterious darkness of

the forest there is the other world, the magical world in which witches, helpful birds, untold treasures, and lots of other things exist.

If we again translate this motif into the realm of the soul, our consciousness can be substituted for the real everyday world, and our unconscious for the marvelous, magical world. We really cannot overlook the fact that all these remarkable and improbable things that come to pass there occur just as much in our dreams and fantasies, i.e., in the manifestations of our unconscious. Within this realm in this fairy tale, there rules the witch, one of the most important major figures of the magical realm, whom we will discuss in greater detail later. Again and again we find this figure, sometimes as witch, sometimes as Spider Woman in North American tales, or as Baba Yaga in Russian stories, sometimes as a female demon or as a goddess, as ancestor, as grandmother, or even as only an old woman who commands a deeper knowledge of nature—like the old woman in "The Worn-out Shoes" who tells the soldier how he can find out what the princesses do at night. She is part good, part evil, a problem we touched on earlier when considering Frau Holle, and hence she embodies an archetypal mother figure who possesses a superior knowledge and superior powers, who can approach humans in part helpfully and generously, in part demoniacally and destructively. She has her mythological parallels in the great nature goddesses of pre-Christian religions and thus personifies a deeper, more powerful natural force that far surpasses the human conscious ego.

Here reflection shows us clearly that our conscious ego is by no means always master in its own house, but that we humans are controlled by deep emotional forces which we know how to deal with only inadequately. When things go well, we can become the servants of beneficently creative and productive forces; when things go badly we become the exponents of dark, demonic drives such as power lust and destructive rage.

But let us now try to bring these mythological images we have been discussing back into our day-to-day existence. To do this we need to look back to the very beginnings of human development. Initially the child is both psychically and physically a unity with the mother, and only gradually in the course of many years of development does the child experience a more or less successful separation, individuation, and independence from this unitary state. Today we know that this process must not be skewed too much in either one or the other direction without seriously damaging the child. Independence achieved too early—the mother's absence in the extreme case of the hospitalized child—causes psycho-physical development to cease and to regress (as the work of, especially, R. Spitz has shown [1965]). On the other hand, "too much mother" results in damage to the child's independence and individuation. Through these given facts of human development the "maternal factor," if I may call it that, receives a negative or a positive character for the child, depending on the specific situation.

Translated into an everyday scenario it might look like this: A child has developed to the point that it can undertake the first excursions into the world, as in, for instance, going to the store all alone to buy a lollipop. Before the child sets out, it wins a major victory: It must overcome its fear and the yearning that accompanies that fear. It is the yearning to be safe, to let itself be fed, to stay at home. If the child gives in and says, "No, I don't want to go," then the witch has grabbed it, and the child sits like Hansel behind bars. But if it goes forth, it may perhaps come into conflict with the witch again. As a society we are not very friendly to children, and in the store often no one pays the child any attention. Inconsiderately, adults crowd ahead of it. Again the child must overcome its fear, and with the fear also the impulse to run home and hide under mother's apron. The child must make itself noticed, must deal with the merchant, and exchange the tightly clutched coin for the lollipop. If the child is able to do all this, then it has again overcome the witch, its distress is at an end, it can carry home the treasure, i.e., the lollipop. Here again what the fairy tale calls "witch" is the deep, instinctive impulse to prefer a comfortable, warm nest to the battle for the world, and it is really the fairy tale that portrays so trenchantly what takes place behind the façade of such wishes for comfort and shelter.

Thus we would find a second answer to the question of the psychological significance of the fairy tale for the child: The child must learn to come to terms with the reality of deeply instinctive drives in its own nature and must maintain its ego in the face of these often superior forces. In this endeavor, fairy tales offer the child typical possibilities and models in imagistic-symbolic form for surviving in this battle.

If, from this viewpoint, we consider a motif such as burning the witch in the oven, it gains a different, deeper meaning, just as the so-called cruelty of nature is usually much less cruel than what the supposedly civilized human being does. The oven is, for its part, again a womb symbol from which bread is born crisp and brown. The path from the production of the grain to the baking of bread is a path of the transformation of a natural product into a specifically human form of nourishment. Thus the oven is simultaneously a symbol of transformation in which one form of natural energy is reshaped into something humanly edible. The statement of the fairy tale would then run that the negative-demonic side of the maternal drive ground is ready for a metamorphosis and it should be experienced. Quite typically, at the same moment the witch is burned, the stepmother in the fairy tale also disappears, which alludes to the secret connection of this problem in the conscious and the unconscious. If the conscious situation of impoverishment and having no new experiences can be made, then life stagnates and starves. Then it is even necessary that an inducement appear such as the stepmother who thrusts the children into the wealth of the unconscious world.

On this level we can understand the white bird, too, with its delightful song. In dreams, birds very often stand for thoughts, fantasies, intuitive ideas, or intellectual contents. Now white is actually the color of faith, salvation, peace, and joy. One would actually expect that it might have been a black messenger of calamity that would guide and entice the children to follow it to the house of the witch—a negative, dark, and evil idea. But that is not the case. The fairy tale is justifiably of the opinion that it is a splendid idea to meet the gingerbread witch and to come to terms with her, and we can support this view unreservedly.

There is something similar about Hansel's pebbles and bread crumbs. If we cleave to the rigid and dead—the stone—then, indeed, we always again come back, but nothing at all changes. The old cares, the old hungers remain always as they were. There are many grown persons, too, who continually strew pebbles if they happen to do or think something, and who never get out of the habitual. But when the bread, the product of transformation, as we saw earlier, is strewn, something happens. This symbol vanishes from consciousness, only later to turn up again in the form of the oven.

The longer that one contemplates and meditates on fairy tales, the more one occupies oneself with them, and the more they open up and reveal hidden nuances and subtleties that one had earlier overlooked. Hansel and Gretel are abandoned and thrust upon a path. They cry bitterly and do not at all want to enter this uncanny, strange world from which alone their redemption can ultimately come. Is that not our human fate at countless junctures? In this context I recall Klaus Kammers's magnificent rendition of Kafka's "Report to an Academy." There Kafka depicts the course of becoming human which an ape suffering the bitterest straits and torments voluntarily/involuntarily undergoes. Necessity, as one of the greatest taskmistresses of mankind, also leads the involuntary heroes in the fairy tale to their task. From a great many fairy tales and myths we know this profoundly human motif of the normal, fearful person whom fate alone forces to become a hero and who would only all too gladly run away. We need think only of the beautiful story of Jonah and the whale in the Bible.

Concerning the end of this fairy tale there is still one more thing to be said. There we encounter the astonishing fact that on the children's way home the entire landscape has obviously changed. Where previously a transitionless intermingling of the two worlds obtained and the normal world of the woodcutter simply turned into the magical region, now a great, broad body of water separates the two realms. Only with the help of the duck and Gretel's reasoning are the two children in a position to return to everyday life. Here the image expresses a condition which, in contrast with the beginning of the fairy tale, clearly represents psychological progress. We find a lack of delineation between consciousness and the unconscious primarily in a still immature and labile ego. Such persons are handed over to all affects, moods, impulses, and instinctual needs that arise out of the unconscious psyche. They live at the level of *participation mystique* (Levy-Bruhl, 1966) with these unconscious contents. Their egos are handed over to them, are flooded by them, or fall completely under their spell. In the case of the stable and healthy ego, on the other hand, there exists a clear boundary between the two realms. The ego is in the position of deciding which emerging impulses, which needs, etc., should be accepted and executed and which not. Only after the magical, evil, and negative side of the unconscious—the witch—has been overcome does this clear boundary arise. An animal like the duck, which is capable of living in two realms, air and water, may then be the appropriate symbol for the mediator between these two worlds. Thus it becomes the fitting vehicle for what can and may come across and for what must be turned away from consciousness.

I am well aware that I have only hinted at a small part of what is contained in such a fairy tale. Every work of art—and the fairy tale is a work of art—shaped by an entire people is fundamentally inexhaustible and broad like the form-giving, creative matrix of the soul itself. I wanted only to stimulate the reader to reflect on what thoughts and ideas one can have concerning such a creation; what effects on the soul such a dynamic sequence of images can release. It is a sequence that contains experiences of depth psychology, experiences that are now today being described in rational-abstract-scientific concepts.

What today may be our most modern experiences, the fairy tale has known since ancient times. Only it speaks in a different, very simple and simultaneously very difficult and very deep language of pictures.

CHAPTER 4

Fairy-Tale Motifs in Dreams and Fantasies

In the preceding chapter the starting point of our reflections was the fairy tale, and we related its plot to modes of emotional experience; now we shall take the opposite path. In this chapter our basic materials are the dreams, fantasies, memories, and associations of patients who completed psychotherapeutic treatment for an emotional illness. Starting from products of fantasy we shall show parallels to the fairy-tale materials.

The abundance of mythologems and fairy-tale themes in the unconscious fantasies of people, as the works of Freud (1953–74) and Rank (1926) in particular demonstrate, had already caught the attention of the early psychoanalysts. But only in the work of C. G. Jung and his followers was this mythological level of the unconscious given a special appreciation. According to Jung's view, there exists, so to speak, beneath the personal memories and imaginal contents, a layer of commonly shared, human developmental possibilities, given as inherent natural tendencies and clothed in the world of images corresponding to the culture. Jung calls this layer the collective unconscious. The language of the collective unconscious is that of the world of mythological, primordial images, and it can, if rightly understood, direct the individual to modes of experiencing and to possibilities of emotional functioning which lie outside the range of his personal experience. Concerning this Jung writes:

> We can distinguish a *personal unconscious*, comprising all the acquisitions of personal life, everything forgotten, repressed, subliminally perceived, thought, felt. But, in addition to these personal unconscious contents, there are other contents which do not originate in personal ac-

quisitions but in the inherited possibility of psychic functioning in general, i.e., in the inherited structure of the brain. These are the mythological associations, the motifs and images that can spring up anew anytime anywhere, independently of historical tradition or migration. I call these contents the *collective unconscious*. Just as conscious contents are engaged in a definite activity, so too are the unconscious contents, as experience confirms. And just as conscious psychic activity creates certain products, so unconscious psychic activity produces dreams, *fantasies* (q.v.), etc. (1913, par. 842)

This deep emotional layer of primordial images is always touched whenever an external or internal situation can no longer be comprehended or resolved with the customary modes of experiencing, attitudes, and means learned and practiced heretofore. Basically every neurosis presents just such an insoluble inner and outer problem, and the more severe and deep-seated it is, the more frequent are the often unusual, bizarre, cosmic, and mythological motifs that arise from the unconscious. What is true for the emotional illness that signifies a "stuckness" in such a problematic crisis also holds true in the case of the healthy person for the crisis situations that appear normally in every life. Every person has had the experience of severe inner or outer distress in which the "most improbable" ideas and fantasies occur to them. One has heavy, restless dreams of dark, shadowy content which are so strange that one does not understand them at all. If all goes well, a solution or an idea of which one would never have thought crystallizes out of all this. It points to a way totally unknown up until now and of whose possibilities one knew absolutely nothing. One does not know precisely how this all comes about. As a rule one accepts it, justifiably, as a gift from one's inner nature. Only the psychotherapist who is familiar with these occurrences and also has the corresponding knowledge of mythology knows that these bizarre dreams and fantasies contain mythological motifs in which the possibility of a solution already lies hidden. To speak in images, the soul has, as it were, consulted an old wise person who dwells within us and asked how humankind always has or always could solve such problems, and there has been an answer. Again and again the difficulty, of course, lies in correctly understanding this voice out of one's own depths and also in wanting to understand it; for many times what is said seems to consciousness most disagreeable, unpleasant, or even anxiety producing (cf. "The Snake").

I would now like to give an example which demonstrates this capacity of the soul and which makes clear how a problem should initially be ap-

proached with the "conventional methods." Only when they prove unsuit-
able does emotional energy flow into a deeper level and carry mytholo
gems back up to the surface. For the dreamer these mythologems hold the
possibility of a solution. The example comes from a thirty-seven-year-old
woman who had the following dream at the beginning of psychotherapeutic treatment:

> I am in session with my doctor and we agree on a time for the
> next consultation. We are in a room adjacent to the consultation
> room. Then we were holding hands. I became active and tenderly
> pressed them, but I feel guilty as I do so. Then my doctor's wife
> suddenly came in and said, "The air here is terrible, just as if a
> heat lamp had been on," and she opened the window. Then I was
> suddenly in the right consultation room and it was like a lake. The
> doctor's head was swimming in this lake in a glass bowl, and he
> said that I had to realize I couldn't expect to get a man because
> I was not attractive, not young enough, and did not try hard
> enough. Then the head changed and became an aquatic plant
> that swelled up with water. Then my doctor's two young daugh-
> ters were also there, and the three of us swam around this plant,
> ceremoniously and carefully lifted it up out of the water with our
> hands and set it in the sun so that it would again spread out. The
> whole thing was accompanied with religious feelings as if there
> were something divine about the plant.

First of all we must say something about the dreamer's situation and
problems.

She was a divorced woman and had no children. Two attempts at marriage had failed, and at this time she was asking herself if she should not
once again pull together all her energy and courage and dare another try.
She had an artistic-creative calling to which she was very devoted and into
which, during recent years, she had poured her whole soul. She had felt
strong doubts whether that had been right and was overwhelmed with
considerable fears of loneliness and insecurity. Driven by these fears she
seriously considered marrying a man in the circle of her acquaintances and
leaving her profession. Her fears caused her also to feel insecure in her
professional life.

Very enigmatically the dream discusses the problem of the man-woman
relationship, employing the figure of the analyst. It begins by working with
"conventional" means: man and woman, the doctor and the patient meet-

ing each other in an emotionally close relationship. At first the patient re-
acts simply as a woman. It is the customary and usual continuation of the
man-woman relationship that, following the establishment of felt emotional harmony, the situation becomes erotic. But that obviously isn't appropriate here. She has guilt feelings, expressed in the dream in the figure
of the doctor's wife, who characterizes the situation aptly as smelling bad
and as artificial (the heat lamp). The flood of feelings and the emotional
energy seek, but do not find, discharge in the usual channels. It is interrupted, dammed up, flows back again, and must seek another way. Already at the beginning the dream nicely states that this is not the right way,
for it places the entire scene in a room adjacent to the consultation room.

There now follows a new attempt, and this time it takes place in the right
consultation room. The emotional energy has flowed into the collective images, and the situation which the patient's dream-ego now experiences
becomes fairy tale-like. It all takes place in a world under water. All that
remains is the doctor's head, which obviously makes very hard and unpleasant comments to her, and finally is transformed into a water plant
about which nixies or nymphs swim, and which is lifted out of the water
into sunlight in a sort of birth process. But this time the light is the real, natural sun and no heat lamp, no mechanical apparatus which one can turn
off or on. The feeling qualities that accompany it, too, have changed. What
previously was affection has now become something religious.

Initially the dreamer was perplexed by these "abstruse" ideas, as she
called them. But with the necessary knowledge of the human collective
soul, a fully comprehensible meaning can be found in them. The prophe-
sying, speaking head is found in many fairy tales, be it as an animal head
as in the "The Goose Girl" of the Brothers Grimm (Manheim, 1983), or
the human head in the South American tale "The Moon" (Koch-Grünberg, ed., 1921), or in the Eskimo tale "The Death's Head" (Rasmussen,
ed., 1937). All these tales are concerned with a speaking skull that obviously has secret natural knowledge at its disposal. This corresponds to the
fact that among a great many peoples the head is viewed as the locus of
the soul or of the center of life, and hence also can contain the entire being
and knowledge of the person whose head it is. According to Levy-Bruhl
(1966), the natives of New Guinea preserve the skulls of the deceased,
decorate them, and call them "korwars." In the skull, so they believe,
dwells the soul of the deceased, and no native facing an important decision
will neglect to explain his plan in detail to the skull and to ask it for advice.

If we apply these ideas to the dream, the primitive, natural soul dwelling in this woman reduces the doctor to the symbol of a head possessing the oracular qualities known from fairy tales and myths. To the head she tells her plan of getting married, so to speak, and the head prophesies that her plan is senseless because it could not succeed. That she is no longer young corresponds to the facts; nevertheless she is otherwise a distinctly attractive woman. The hard statement that she is not attractive enough would then have more the meaning that it would be misdirected effort to invest her energies in external attractiveness. Obviously this head does not think much of her all-too-understandable wishes and advises her against squandering her attention and energy in this direction. Of course, the doctor himself does not give any advice in therapy, but here we are dealing with a spontaneous product of the patient's unconscious, that is to say, with advice that the unconscious gives to consciousness.

After this has happened, the patient joins the "Daughters of the Head," which would correspond to the ego's turning toward this inner natural soul. Then the transformation takes place. The nixies or nymphs that have appeared are known to us from countless stories: according to the attitude or situation in which one encounters them, they appear as helpful or also partially dangerous nature beings. It is a question of a deep part of female nature which, in its tendency to surface and to strive toward the sun, is reminiscent of the beautiful tale by Andersen, "The Mermaid" (1978). In the form of the youngest daughter of a Sea King, Andersen has expressed nature's inherent deep longing for consciousness which alone imparts an immortal soul. (This tale and the motif of the nymphs or nixies will be discussed in detail in Chapter 5 in connection with the favorite childhood fairy tale.)

We find a similar longing to become conscious in the well-known romantic story, "Undine," by de la Motte Fouque (n.d.). Undine, too, is the daughter of a Sea King and likewise has the unconquerable yearning for a soul. Consequently she falls into the hands of a fisherman and his wife who rear her. During a storm a knight seeks shelter in their hut and she charms him with her beauty. A priest, conveniently also driven to the hut by the storm, weds the couple. She confesses to her husband that she has no soul and implores him never to say a cross word to her when close to water lest the inhabitants of that element fetch her back.

The knight takes her to his castle, but naturally he is plagued by good Christian mistrust, and, as fate would have it, there appears another beautiful woman, Berthalda, who hopes to become the knight's wife. Now Undine seems ever more uncanny to the knight, and, while during a jour-

ney by boat she retrieves a coral necklace from the water rather than Berthalda's necklace which had fallen in, he calls her a witch and a sorceress.
In tears Undine leaps overboard and vanishes in her element, but not without warning the knight to remain faithful to her as the water people would
otherwise take revenge.

But the knight pays no heed to the warning and after a time prepares to
wed Berthalda. On the day of the wedding she has beauty water fetched
from the castle well which Undine had had sealed up. When the stone cov-
ering the well is raised, Undine's spirit rises out of it and goes to the knight
and embraces him. He dies from her kiss.

Here the acquisition of a soul is not linked to the wedding as such, but
rather to the lasting bond of marriage, and both founder when it is not
kept. In this story the dangerous and the beneficent sides of this female
creature of nature are united in one figure.

But let us return to the dream of my patient. Obviously as consciousness
sinks back into this deep, unconscious layer of the feminine natural soul, a
transformation and a process of birth directed toward the sun is released
by the symbol of the head. As the patient herself said, it was a religious
phenomenon. Hence it seems appropriate to seek an analogy to this note-
worthy plant birth from the religious realm. In the West we scarcely know
the motif of the flower birth; but in the East, especially in Buddhism, it is
well known, and there are many stories of the Buddha's birth from a lotus.

In "The Life and Teachings of Tibet's Great *Guru* Padma-Sambhava,"
the lotus birth of Buddha is described:

> On his return to the Urgyan country, just as the minister Trigunadhara ap-
> proached and greeted him, the King noticed a rainbow of five colours
> over the Dhanakosha Lake, although there were no clouds and the sun
> was shining brightly. . . .
>
> The King and his minister went to the lake and, taking a small boat,
> reached the place over which the rainbow shone. There they beheld a
> fragrant lotus blossom, the circumference of which exceeded that of one's
> body and circled arms, and seated at the centre of the blossom a fair rosy-
> cheeked little boy resembling the Lord Buddha, holding in his right hand
> a tiny lotus blossom and in his left hand a tiny holy-water pot, and in the
> folds of the left arm a tiny three-pronged staff.
>
> The King felt much veneration for the self-born babe; and, in excess of
> joy, he wept. He asked the child, "Who are thy father and mother, and of
> what country and caste art thou? What food sustaineth thee; and why art

thou here?" The child answered, "My father is Wisdom and my mother is the Voidness. My country is the country of the *Dharma*. I am of no caste and of no creed. I am sustained by perplexity; and I am here to destroy Lust, Anger, and Sloth." Overwhelmed with joy, the King named the child "The Lakeborn *Dorje*," and he and the minister made obeisance to the child.

The meaning and the content of this lotus birth is a religious figure, a Buddha, whose tasks lie not in the biological but in the culturally creative field. His energies do not flow into starting a family and securing a means of livelihood but in preaching a doctrine which is supposed to call forth a general development of humanity. It may seem presumptuous to insert such a great and momentous image into the healing process of a neurosis, but in the background of many of these illnesses there lies hidden just such a problem concerned with the very meaning and the basis of human life itself.

Fate had denied this woman the fulfillment of her rightful biological wishes, as it has so many. Her own unconscious tells her that it no longer makes sense to try to force once again the course of her life in this direction. Instead, it points her in a different direction. In the language of these mythological, fabulous images it shows consciousness a path which, on the one hand, demands sacrifice and renunciation but which, on the other hand, can find its own happiness in the culturally creative act. It is an "as if" in which the religious personality stands as a model of her own, very much more limited, possibilities.

As already mentioned, in her profession the patient had the possibility of generally valuable cultural creative activity. Basically the unconscious affirms her being, but simultaneously it reveals to her a deeper aspect of her activity to which she had not paid sufficient attention heretofore. She had entered her profession quite unconsciously. At first she had regarded it more as a job that one has to have to earn a living. Securing her own livelihood and earning recognition had stood in the foreground. If she understood the image of her dream and accepted it, it could give her activity a new, deeper meaning and content and thus free her from her doubts.

Naturally it is always an open question whether or not the person concerned takes this stance. The imaginal world of the unconscious speaks to us; now we can attempt to understand this language and carefully include its contents in our deliberations. But we do not have to. There are many people who live oblivious of themselves, who understand little of what their own nature tells them, or who pay no heed at all. For the most part that happens at their own expense and leads to failures, outer and inner conflicts, or to sickness. Mere understanding does not suffice either, but rather the carefully weighed compromise between consciousness and the unconscious must be achieved in an often long and laborious process. So did it came about in the case described here. The patient set out successfully upon the path suggested by the unconscious so that the symptomatology of her illness gradually improved.

Let us now look at another dream of a different patient. This time it is a young man of twenty-two who had a dream toward the end of his treatment. The figure with whom he comes to terms here is the generally known figure of the witch, whom we already met with Hansel and Gretel and whom we meet here in a different form. Next to the evil giant, the magician, the nixie, and the dwarf, among others, this fairy-tale creature is one of the most common to occur in the dreams of patients. He reported the following dream:

> I have driven with my sister to a small city and was strolling about in the streets with her. Later I was alone and came into a narrow, medieval street that ran from right to left and went somewhat uphill. I stopped at a magic and antique shop. I went in. The proprietress was rather plump and had a veil in her hair. She was very attractive and looked like a real aristocrat. She showed me her marvelous things very amiably. I saw that she was a witch and persuaded her to teach me magic. She showed me some tricks and made a ball and other things vanish. It was very hard for me to imitate her. I had to balance the ball on a taut string and say "simsalabim" or something like that at the same time. I saw that making magic is difficult. She taught me all sorts of things, and when I had gotten better at it, she took me into her private rooms. There we continued to make magic. Now I was really good at the trick, so good that the witch almost couldn't get the ball back again. Then we discovered it in the radiator, and I had to wind a string tightly around the ball. When I was finished she said to me that it was a piece of world that I had created. I doubted that, but she went on with the agenda and entered something in her book.

This young man had been a lively and robust child. When he was seven, his father was arrested on political grounds and did not return to the family until eight years later. After this event, the mother experienced severe anxiety states which seriously inhibited this boy's healthy expansion. He was not permitted to go out alone and always had to stay home evenings. Even when he was older, he always had to tell where he had been or where he was going. So he had become a loner who stayed at home too much and sank into unproductive day-dreaming. Although he understood his mother's problems, when he came for treatment he had a quite negative-rejecting attitude toward everything maternal-feminine since this, of course, meant to him imprisonment in an area of fear. Of course he thereby also denied an essential part of his own nature for the human being is after all a product of both father and mother. As a consequence of this he was possessed by intense feelings of inferiority, accompanied by severe disturbance in his ability to work and the inability to choose a profession.

In the course of treatment, he had gained a degree of energetic masculinity that helped him to be able to assert himself against the negative, entrapping, maternal anxiety. Toward the end of treatment he once again addressed the problem with his mother after having had the dream given above. Behind the previously demonic-witch-like area of anxiety he now discovered a different side of his own inner nature which he had rejected up until now. Earlier he had always said, "People like me don't amount to anything." But now he ascertained that he had a quite valuable gift for music and a considerable talent in drawing. His musical component came from his mother's side of the family. Now he developed it, and he decided to study at a well-known art academy where he easily passed the entrance exams.

As already mentioned, the dream introduced this development. The sorceress, who still carried something of the evil, entrapping witch experienced earlier, now teaches him to create a piece of world for which the ball is a clear symbol. At the time of the dream he himself did not want to believe and accept that. Hence at the end of the dream he is shown still doubting. "Great Mother Nature," symbolized in the witch who places her gifts and abilities at the disposal of him who learns and puts some effort into working with her, takes little heed of his doubts and obviously inscribes his further path, about which she already knows with certainty, in the book of fate.

At the word "witch" we are usually accustomed to think initially of the evil witch from "Hansel and Gretel." But just as common in the fairy tale is the motif of a magical, benevolent mother figure who richly rewards those who are of service to her. If we juxtapose these two sides of the Great

Mother in nature, the fairy-tale figures that most closely correspond to them are Mother Holle on the one hand and the witch in "Hansel and Gretel" on the other.

In the tale "Mother Holle," a widow has two daughters of whom the one, the real daughter, is lazy and very fond of fine clothes, and the other is diligent but treated as a stepchild, a "Cinderella." She must sit all day at the well and spin until her hands are bloody, and when her spindle once accidentally falls into the well, she is so frightened that she jumps in after it to fetch it back again. There below she comes to a meadow where an oven implores her to remove the fresh baked bread, and an apple tree wants her to shake its ripe apples off. The girl does both and finally arrives at the house of Mother Holle, an old woman with large teeth, of whom she is afraid. But Mother Holle is friendly and invites her in, and the girl goes into service with her to clean her house and make her bed. When she shakes the bedding and the feathers fly, it snows in the world. After she has served diligently for a period of time, she asks to return to the upper world, and Mother Holle leads her to a great gate. When she opens it, a rain of gold falls upon the girl so that she returns home richly rewarded.

Now of course the lazy sister wants to try the same thing, jumps in the well, but ignores the oven and the tree and arrives at Mother Holle's. Only with great difficulty does she succeed in working the first day, and then she again gets lazy until Mother Holle has finally had enough of that and dismisses her. She, too, is led to the gate, but now instead of gold it rains down pitch, which sticks so tightly to her that it can't be removed as long as she lives.

In this tale we again have the two realms, the everyday realm of consciousness and the magical realm of the unconscious, which can be reached here through the well and which lies below the earth. The timelessness and spacelessness of the unconscious and the inversion of above and below in the fairy tale are very nicely depicted in the fact that it snows up above when down below the feather bedding is shaken. In the soul, too, there is, after all, basically no above or below. When we use an expression such as that of "depth" for emotional things, we are transferring a concept from our spatial world to a non-spatial dimension. The central figure of this magical realm is Mother Holle, the image of a nature goddess who rules over the elements. Exactly as in the patient's dream she still has, even for the diligent girl who gets the gold, a bit of the negative-demonic aspect of the witch, as imaged by her long teeth. She also reveals this destructive-negative aspect vis-à-vis the lazy girl; for only zealous efforts, diligence, and genuine interest can bring the valuable sides of the unconscious to bear. A violently egotistical and lazy attitude that wants to exploit the energies contained in the unconscious is usually condemned to failure and ends up with a run of bad luck.

The oven, the first thing the girl meets, may well be one of the oldest transformation symbols of humanity. Here we can append some further reflections on this symbol. If we try to imagine ourselves in the situation of primal man, then we can gauge what a tremendous discovery it must have been to transform grain into edible and tasty bread. In this act lies hidden our earliest ancestors' emotional achievement of renouncing and reshaping a drive before which we have every reason to feel limitless respect. What must it have cost early man to bear the most violent and most threatening drive, hunger, in a long and hard winter without devouring the seed corn, and to develop the condition of his consciousness from instant gratification to long-range planning? Thus the oven, which in form and function also corresponds to the symbol of a nurturing womb furthering the processes of maturation, stands at the border of the magical realm of the "Great Mother." Whoever passes it by cannot expect to succeed in anything. In the Demeter cult in Greece the grain of wheat is the "child" of the goddess of the grain. It was called "the strong" because human strength has its origin in bread (Harding, 1948). Nature herself cannot befriend one who cannot even take the trouble to collect her ripe fruits, such as are offered in the apple tree, and thus she falls victim to her demonic side.

We find this most explicitly in the tale of "Hansel and Gretel," discussed earlier. But some additional observations and reflections are still necessary here.

The end of "Hansel and Gretel" is actually very immoral in terms of our concepts, for the father, who was too weak to resist the evil suggestion of his wife and with her abandoned the children in the forest, is not only *not* punished for his highly immoral way of acting but *even* gets to enjoy the treasures the children bring back. He is, as it were, rewarded for his feeble behavior; for, had he not followed the evil advice of his wife, he would probably have remained as poor as before. Fairy tales, however, are not geared to the customary problems of our civilized human consciousness but are a sort of dream of humankind. The fairy tale cares just as little for the usual ethical norms in consciousness as do our dreams. Consequently

M.-L. von Franz speaks of an ethos of the unconscious, of nature itself, concerned with the "right" attitude that leads to a happy end in contrast to a wrong attitude that leads to misfortune (1983).

Actually the entire ambiguity of our problem of good and evil lies hidden in this tale. In *Faust*, Mephistopheles expresses it when he says he is "A part of that power/That always wants evil and always creates good." In the fairy tale it is actually the evil spirit of the stepmother that possesses the father and that finally brings about the redemption of the family from its poverty-stricken condition. While the benevolent aspect of the mother stills the hunger and rewards efforts, the evil mother uses just these drives to lure the child on and then to hold it prisoner (Hansel), as well as exploit its ability to work and its productivity (Gretel) for the satisfaction of her own egotistical drives.

Vanquishing this overwhelming demonic force succeeds here through cunning, a mode of action of which the fairy tale is obviously very fond —consider the tales called "Peasants and Devils" or "The Brave Little Tailor" —and which often leads to success. It appears that in her captivity in the negative mother complex, as we would call it psychologically, Gretel has learned something from it; for it was with cunning, after all, that the witch herself lured the children into her realm. In this motif lies hidden something of the fairy tale's knowledge of these overwhelming natural forces for which the strength of the individual human being simply is no match. Thus in his battle for survival, we must sometimes employ sneaky and underhanded tactics. Evil then, so to speak, vanquishes itself and is burned up in the oven.

Frequently such dreams of the evil, entrapping witch in the forest are told by patients in psychotherapeutic treatment as memories from childhood. For example, a twenty-four-year-old woman told me that when she was between ten and eleven years old she dreamed that she came into a forest, and suddenly the trees would no longer let go of her. There had been witches there who had continued to lure her onward and had commanded the trees not to let her flee under any conditions. This dream had impressed her so powerfully that she had even written a school essay about it.

Of course, one can say that the child was so powerfully impressed or frightened by a fairy tale it heard or read—such as "Hansel and Gretel" —that it simply reproduced it. Opposing this, however, is the fact that in the course of a single day we are exposed to an almost infinite number of perceptions and impressions. Hence the question remains open why precisely this dream is selected while other things that are perhaps empirically much more frightening are laid aside as unimpressive. Insofar as one takes the trouble to look for them, one can regularly find clear connections between such fairy-tale motifs and the personal problems of the child in question. So it was in this case.

The patient, a girl, had at a very early age lost her father in the war and had grown up an only child with her mother. From her eighth to her tenth year she was severely ill with tuberculosis and was confined to bed in a hospital for several months. After her discharge, her mother and those around her anxiously made certain that she moved about as little as possible. Among the sad experiences of her childhood that she again and again recalled in treatment was the memory of having to lie quietly on a blanket in the shade in a meadow while all the other children were allowed to romp and play unrestrained around her. She then frantically tried with all possible cunning and tricks to lure one of the children to her blanket so that it would remain and play with her, but she seldom had any luck. So in this situation, her own illness and the concern of those about her were, on the one hand, the entrapping witch, and on the other hand she herself had become partially identified with the witch in that she attempted to catch the other children and keep them for herself.

In the session in which this long-forgotten dream from her childhood again emerged from the unconscious, its relationship to her own fate and also to her present illness became apparent for the first time. She had come because of severe depressions and difficulties in working. Now she recalled that for a long time following her earlier illness she had had a terrible fear of relapsing, of again falling ill. She had never dared really to play with the other children and had become a loner, to which a number of additional factors had also contributed. Even in her present depression, in her current inability for constructive work and movement, there still lay the same old, deep fear and uncertainty about her own physical nature to which the drives and instincts of the unconscious also belonged. Since all consciousness arises only from the unconscious, and the body is the material (Latin *mater* = mother) of her mankind, there exists a connection with the experience of an image of the Great Mother, who for this patient had magically entrapping and clinging characteristics. Here we are dealing with the transpersonal significance of the figure of the mother who, just like the personal mother, possesses a negative side in her desire to to hold on to the child. Thus the witch expresses a death aspect of mother nature who with her frightening side again destroys what she herself has given birth to and takes it back into herself. A correspondingly dark effect always emanates from the unconscious since every increase in maturation and consciousness comes about only with effort and against the resistance of the unconscious. And the unconscious again and again threatens to eclipse or to devour the newly gained consciousness, which unfortunately happens only all too often when the ego is weak during a physical illness.

The extent to which the patient was exposed to this danger is shown in a dream from the early phase of her treatment. Moreover, this dream casts a light on the motif of the person banished in animal form with which we are already familiar from the first fairy tale about the snake. The patient dreamed:

> My feet are hurt and I am dancing about in a room. Somebody, who himself is a tiger, says to me, "Why don't we change ourselves into predators, then we will no longer notice our illness." But I don't do it.

First of all, this dream reminded her of the tale by Andersen, "The Little Mermaid" (1978), already mentioned earlier. In Andersen's tale it is one of the characteristics of the Sea Princess that her new feet, which grew out of the fish tail, hurt her greatly when she runs or dances, as if they were being pierced by sharp swords. The process of acquiring a human soul, i.e., maturation and consciousness, is here obviously linked with suffering and pain. During this time the patient took the first laborious and often still unsuccessful steps toward getting out of her neurosis. In addition to her depressions, accumulated violent drives and affects erupted, leaving her feeling somewhat relieved but placing her in impossible situations. These situations couldn't be reconciled with the "upper" human side of her personality. In the dream for the first time she wards off the temptation arising from her own soul to withdraw from her suffering by becoming compulsive, letting her self go, and reducing her consciousness to an animal level. The predatory animal symbolizes the unconscious instinctuality of her own nature which threatened to extinguish her human ego.

Now we recall that just such instinctuality was also the sin of the prince who was transformed into a snake in our first fairy tale and who needed to be redeemed by the girl. In that tale his transformation was the consequence of a curse because he had seduced an orphan. Thus this dream of a contemporary individual casts light on the ancient motif of the person fallen victim to his own animal instinctuality and on the origin of this motif.

In order to express the extraordinary complexity, the compounding of the most diverse elements, and the distance from or foreignness to consciousness of a complex, the unconscious often reaches back to the images of fantastic zoology in myth and fairy tale. Then in our dreams the sphinx, the unicorn, the phoenix, the griffin, harpies, centaurs, or similar monsters appear, and the dreamer must come to terms with them. Again an example will illustrate this.

The following dream comes from a twenty-eight-year-old woman and was dreamed shortly after beginning psychotherapy:

> I am walking with my boyfriend across planks in water that is partly shallow, partly deep. A path runs beside the water, but there was a swarm of bees there, and that's why we were walking on the planks. When we got back to land again, the swarm was gone. Then we came to a large, castle-like house; to the right stood a tower, which tapered toward the top and had lots of windows; but everything was burned out and gone to ruin. We went around it. There was supposed to be a pastor's family living there. Behind the house lay a garden. In it we saw a griffin which lay an egg like a hen, and we laughed about it. The griffin didn't like that and ran after us.
>
> Then my friend was suddenly no longer there. I crawled off into a house with no windows. But the griffin could get in there, too; besides me there was a blonde girl and a wolf in there. The griffin wanted to kill me, and the girl and the wolf gave me good advice: I shouldn't eat anything, but leave everything for the bird. Then I made him (the griffin) something to eat from an onion. I crawled into the top drawer of a kitchen cabinet. Over my head there was yet another drawer; in it was the food that he always ate. When he came the third time, I gave him honey. I had a sweet taste in my mouth and didn't like it that I had eaten the same thing he had. Then he came once again, and I felt his hot breath above my head.
>
> He dragged me out. Now he had become a wolf and said to me, "That is a wonderful chamberpot." I was the chamberpot; I had long, ornate Rococo arms and legs. Then I murdered the wolf by choking off his air. Meanwhile he had become a marten. I was surprised how easily it went. Then for safety's sake I stuck him in a pot of boiling water, and it was again the griffin. When I finally had the griffin in the kettle, I knew that there was yet a third test.

It is not possible here to discuss in detail this colorful dream so rich in symbols; we must confine ourselves to the central problem, the dreamer's struggles with the griffin.

In connection with this dream the patient was reminded of the Grimms' tale "The Griffin," which had made a strong impression on her as a girl. In this fairy tale the daughter of a king is seriously ill. "Stupid Hans," the youngest of a peasant's three sons, succeeds in healing the King's daughter after his two older and smarter brothers have failed. In order to marry her, however, he must still perform three tasks the king sets; one of the tasks is that of getting a feather from the tail of the Griffin. Hans makes a long journey, during which three people ask him to put a question to the Griffin who "knows everything." Finally he reaches the Griffin's house. There he finds a woman, the Griffin's wife, who advises him that "no Christian can talk to the Griffin" and that he should hide under the bed while *she* asks Hans's questions for him. So Hans hides under the Griffin's bed and during the night he plucks a feather from its tail. The Griffin awakens and his wife explains that he must have been having a bad dream, and simultaneously she tricks him into answering the three questions. In the morning Hans returns home and, after tricking the king, marries the king's daughter.

In this fairy tale the griffin is obviously a most malevolent creature dangerous to humans and hostile to Christians. In the almost identical tale of "The Devil with the Three Golden Hairs" (Zaunert, ed., 1958), the hero must enter the cave and there with the help of the devil's grandmother he procures the hairs from the devil himself. We know the symbol of the griffin from pre-Christian times from descriptions in Heroditus and Pliny. The most detailed description comes from Sir John Mandeville in the 85th chapter of his famous journeys:

> Moreover there exist there many griffins, more than elsewhere, and many say the forward part of their bodies is like that of an eagle and the hind part like that of a lion, and this is the truth, for thus are they constituted; but the griffin has a body that is larger than eight lions and it is stronger than a hundred eagles. For there is no doubt that he can fly with a horse and rider to his nest or two yoked oxen when they go to plough the field, for he has talons on his feet as large as the ox's body, and of them men make goblets and from his ribs bows with which to shoot arrows.

In medieval symbolism, this mythological animal appears by no means only as the embodiment of evil and identical with the devil, for it also contains its opposite, as the griffin was taken as a symbol of Christ. Precisely this contrast seems very important to us when we consider what it meant to our patient to come to terms with this inner image.

Regarded psychologically, that which appears here in the image of the griffin obviously represents an unconscious complex of surpassing power. It is an animal and thus is still closely associated with the instinctive, animalistic-natural side of the psyche. Obviously it has to do with a power that is considerably superior to the conscious ego, and before which the dreamer must flee, trembling with fear, and initially hide. Only when other helpful forces appear on the scene—the girl and the wolf—does she succeed in escaping the impending danger of being devoured or swallowed by the complex. In more or less intense form, most people know this sort of condition in which our consciousness fills up with thoughts, ideas, and emotions that we really do not want, that we even reject, and that nevertheless cannot be pushed aside but often exert a pernicious effect, extending into our attitudes and actions.

Now in itself a natural force is neutral, which is just as true for the forces working in us as for those of the outer world. Admittedly, the energies contained in nature take little heed of our moral convictions and our utilitarian concerns. They stand beyond that and are neither good nor evil. They can be both helpful, blessed, and fruitful and also demoniacally destructive, devastating, and fatal. It always depends on what attitude our ego takes toward them, or must take in order to maintain our humanity and our struggle for survival. The ambiguity of the symbol expresses precisely this state of affairs in that the griffin is identical on the one hand with evil and the devil, and on the other can be identical with the highest good and with Christ. If we succeed in establishing a harmonious relationship with the animal energies in us, they constitute for us a highest good out of which life can only then be realized. If on the other hand we come into conflict with them, they with their superior power often become threatening to consciousness and unfortunately often have a devastating effect. It is part of our tragedy that we must always come into such conflict; for we differ from the animal in that we must live not *in* nature but *against* nature. Hence this conflict with our animal nature concerns us all and not only the person suffering with a neurosis; coming to terms with this conflict has a collective validity.

The analysis of this woman, whose personal background we cannot discuss here, confirmed that in the image of the griffin, there was contained a complex of still unmastered drives contaminated with idealizations erected on and about them. Precisely for this reason the griffin was the appropriate image to represent this because as the lion it symbolizes predatory impulses still foreign to the ego; as eagle and winged animal it points to the world of ideas, fantasies, and thoughts, which man has always seen as an analogy to the bird's flight. The dream clearly emphasizes the intimate inner connection of the dreamer with this fabulous creature as she herself has the taste of honey in her mouth when the griffin eats honey.

Now next to the figure of the griffin there is a second, common, and typical fairy-tale motif contained in the dream. This motif is found in the transformation battle that takes place between the dreamer and the fabulous creature. Here the griffin turns into a wolf and then a marten, and only at the end of the story resumes its own form after being killed. Simultaneously the dreamer also is temporarily transformed into the exquisitely poetic Rococo chamberpot. We find such typical contests of transformation, for example, in the fairy tale called "The Sorcerer's Apprentice" (Zaunert, ed., 1958), in which the hero battles against his master, a sorcerer, after having learned magic arts in order to win a princess. There is a variant found in the oriental tales of *The Thousand and One Nights* where, in a contest of transformation, a princess, herself commanding magical powers, redeems the hero bewitched into the form of an ape. This tale comes from the cycle called "The Story of the Porter and the Three Ladies," specifically, "The Tale of the Second Mendicant." I gave this fairy tale a detailed analytical interpretation in my book, *Individuation in the Fairy Tales from 1001 Nights* (Dieckmann, 1974). Likewise we find this motif in *The Odyssey* (Lattimore, trans. 1967). At that point where the goddess Eidothea helps Menelaos and his companions obtain a prophecy about their return home from her father, the sea god Proteus. The text trenchantly depicts his capacities of transformation:

> First he turned into a great bearded lion,
> and then to a serpent, then to a leopard, then to a great boar,
> and he turned into fluid water,
> to a tree with towering branches . . . (p. 177).

Viewed psychologically, in the magical figures' capacities for transformation and in their difficult accessibility and comprehensibility for change lie a clear parallel to the contents of the unconscious which are incapable of consciousness and which are accustomed to appear equally fleeting and mutable in the light of conscious awareness. Now precisely the psychoanalytic process attempts to grasp these very peripheral and fleeting contents and to join them to consciousness. In the dream the ultimate capture of the griffin and plunging him into the kettle where he can be made "edible" correspond to this process. Edible in this instance would mean that the forces and ideas contained in the unconscious complex thoroughly mature and can then be employed consciously. This would be the real task of analysis, and hence the conclusion of the dream offers the possibility for a new beginning.

The space available to us here does not permit going beyond these few examples of fairy-tale motifs in the dreams of modern persons. A series of this sort could be continued indefinitely since there is scarcely an analysis in which the mythological and fairy-tale motifs do not appear in greater or lesser number. In this the creative fantasy of the unconscious usually combines the motifs and the plots of fairy tales we know indiscriminately, just as they correspond to the dreamer's problems in this individual case. Thus the unconscious composes one's own individual fairy tale. For the psychotherapist it is of great value to be familiar with a large number of such archetypal motifs and their symbolic meaning, for this leads to a deepened understanding of the distinct language of the unconscious. Without this knowledge one often overlooks the symbols: one dreams a fairy tale and doesn't even know it. Then one casts this very valuable bit of ancient cultural knowledge aside and behaves like the ignorant Parsifal at his first sojourn in the Grail Castle, again losing the thing of value because he forgot to ask.

For the contemporary person, often technically and rationally oriented, it is a deeply moving experience when such bright, colorful images full of life and mysterious meaning arise from within. A merchant whose ideas and thoughts were filled with numbers, contracts, bids for goods, etc., and who suffered from the feeling of a boring emptiness in his life, began to come to life when in a dream he attempted to cross a river with a dangerous rhinoceros that threatened to devour him. At the moment of greatest peril two swords swam on the water toward him from the left. One of them was an oriental scimitar with which he could defend himself against the monster. He had dreamed the ancient motif of the battle against the dragon, recounted in countless myths and fairy tales, in which a virgin or a treasure beckons the victor. Even though in the dream he never thought of slaying the monster or crossing the river but had to restrict himself to defending himself, he nevertheless grasped that there was more in him than only his business. The image gave him back a bit of trust in other possibilities of his soul which could enliven and beautify his life. The princess or the treasure, the rewards of a successful battle with the dragon in the fairy tale, are the intrapsychic images symbolizing the the discovery of new realms of experience and a fulfilled life. If one has experienced it oneself or with one's patients, one knows what an enrichment of life and how much new joy in living can be won here.

CHAPTER 5

One's Favorite Fairy Tale
from Childhood

Not only the dream containing specific fairy-tale motifs but also certain tales themselves can reveal profound connections with a person's fate, inner world, certain forms of experiencing, illnesses and weaknesses as well as strengths. I am thinking here of a fairy tale or a fairy-tale-like story which fascinated a person in childhood and was a tale especially loved or feared. Later it was forgotten or repressed and thus sank into the unconscious, where, however, it retained a marked vitality and exerted effects that the grown person would never have associated with the tale.

About fifteen years ago I encountered this sort of tale for the first time in the analysis of a patient; it was mentioned almost by chance and in passing. She associated to a somewhat striking and odd dream that the motif reminded her of the beginning of a fairy tale which had greatly fascinated her as a child, so much so that she and some of her girlfriends had enacted it in play. Now, of course, she could scarcely recall the content, nor did she know exactly where in the story the dream motif belonged, but in any case the dream had a definite similarity with the fantasy images that had grown up around the fairy tale at that time. Since as an analyst I had learned to pay serious attention to mythological background elements that appear, I read the fairy tale, which I, too, only vaguely recalled, and I was immediately struck by the many parallels to my patient's fate and experiences, extending even to the symptoms of her illness.

The more I thought about this patient and the fairy tale, the more closely knit, convincing, and numerous the parallels got, so that it became clear that in a certain core sense this young woman had lived not her own life but that of the heroine of a fairy tale. Meanwhile the patient had also reread the tale and had spotted similar parallels, which in part complemented those I had found; she was quite shaken. For a considerable number of analytic hours the fairy tale played a significant role; then again it disappeared under the pressure of current or genetic personal problems; yet from time to time it again emerged from the background, either brought up by her or by one of my interpretations, so that actually during the entire analysis it played a substantial role.

Since having had this experience I began to watch for this phenomenon in other patients, and I soon determined that it was by no means a unique or infrequent occurrence but rather that by far the greater number of my patients mentioned or could find one or two such tales, and that for all these patients there were more or less clearly the same parallels to their psychological dynamics. Naturally the role that this fairy tale played in the course of the analysis differed from patient to patient. For the one it emerged only briefly and the parallels were noted more by me than by the patient; for another it held more the center of our interest for a period of time, as in the first case. Between these extremes there were all possible gradations. What remained essential was that I made it a habit to look for such a favorite tale or most-feared tale from childhood at certain points in the analytic process and according to a specific methodology.

It is by no means the case that the favorite tale always lies close to consciousness, a fact anyone can easily confirm. If one asks a sizable number of persons outright and without analytic preparation, "What really was your favorite childhood fairy tale?" only a small number can give a genuine and honest answer. Usually these stories lie deep in the unconscious, and for this reason alone there arises the question of the method by means of which they can again be made conscious. A further methodological question is that of how these tales can be used therapeutically to further the process of healing and individuation in analytic treatment. These tales fit into the methodology of analytical psychology pretty much on their own and as a matter of course. A number of patients are able to give objective expression to these favorite fairy tales. There are numerous examples of this. The previously mentioned patient, for example, still had drawings from her childhood (age eight to ten) about games on the theme of her fairy tale. Other patients still have stories that they wrote as children about the fairy tale or in which motifs of their fairy tale clearly appear, for example, the puppet show they wrote themselves. A third group still had sketches from their childhood depicting specific motifs from these tales, and a fourth group was able to ask relatives who recalled the patient's fascination about the accuracy of the patient's own memories. Of course these groups are not large; examples of this sort are not all too common and correspondingly they are not statistically relevant. But they do nevertheless speak clearly, if they are at all present, for the objective reality of the favorite fairy tale later mentioned in adult analysis.

A further essential objectivizing factor is direct child observation. On the basis of many years of activity in child analysis and therapy, I was in a position to observe just such fascinating fairy tales also in the analysis particularly of children from four to ten years old. Insofar as fairy tales played any role at all in these cases and were introduced in play therapy by the children, and to the extent that the therapist paid attention or asked about them, the children always had an especially loved or a particularly feared fairy tale. Here, too, there exists the same phenomenon of an intensive relationship between the tale and the child's psychological problems. My most striking memory is the case of a severely disturbed nine-year-old boy in residential placement who had the rather unusual compulsive symptom of pushing in and shattering windows with his bare hand in the treatment facility, at school, and in public buildings. His favorite tale was "The Musicians of Bremen." As is well known, this fairy tale begins with the animals being sent away by their masters because they were useless and only ate, a condition that would correspond to that of a child in a residential treatment setting. The tale has its high point when the animals climb up to an illuminated *window* at the robbers' house, break into the house *through* this window, and hence make the ample meal and the house itself their own, having already chased the robbers away. Such very obvious parallels, which are immediately convincing for even the layperson without interpretation, are, of course, infrequent, although they do also unquestionably occur with adults. Analytical child therapy, as is well known, demands considerable time and sometimes continues over several years, as does adult therapy.

It can often be observed that children change their preferred fairy tale. In by far the greater majority of cases of such a change, however, fairy tales are preferred that center on the same or on similar symbolism, as, for example, "Daumlings Wanderschaft" [Thumbling's Travels] and "The Brave Little Tailor," or "The Seven Ravens" and "The Six Swans." This also supports the view that objectively in the fairy tale quite early on a central complex is structured which can be expressed thus and not otherwise in its essential aspects through more or less exactly determined imagery. These observations were also a further confirmation of the relatively well-accepted Freudian hypothesis that the fundamental psychic structural elements were acquired in the first years of life, and that even in later life the fundamental psychological problems again and again run their course in the framework of these structures or basic complexes.

Early on when I myself was very much fascinated by favorite fairy tales, they dominated the foreground analytically without any conscious intention on my part when working with patients who were especially receptive to these pictures. Without especially forcing my interpretations or hints on them, these patients again and again returned to the fairy tale on their own; they linked it with their problems, also made sketches, paintings, or sculptures connected with it, and repeatedly processed them or worked them through. This is not an especially mysterious occurrence. The particular libidinal interest held by one person colors the atmosphere of a dyadic relationship. Even half-heartedly sensitive patients will "sniff out" where they can awaken the analyst's particular interest and, as a rule, so far as they are not right in the midst of a phase of resistance, will concern themselves with this area. The favorite fairy tale never vanished from my analyses, but eventually it occupied less of a foreground position, especially for the patient.

But the whole thing flared up again for me when I occupied myself with the theme, particularly in publications. Here I must add that for my part I was very cautious and restrained with interpretations and hints, especially after the very first cases had shown me what violent reactions my own strong interest in this area had provoked. From time to time patients even reacted with disappointment and abusive remarks, saying that I did not concern myself enough with their favorite tale; one patient reproached me that I did not even know his favorite fairy tale and had not even thought it necessary to read it, which, in point of fact, was not true.

I believe that this description of the intensity with which a certain psychic realm is evoked in a patient offers a clear indication of the very intensive effect of the subjective factor within countertransference phenomena, regardless of how externally reserved the analyst is. Now such an effect of the subjective factor naturally raises another question: Is what the patient in analysis gives me really "the" favorite fairy tale of childhood or "only" a relatively "chance" choice? (I use quotation marks on "the" and "only" quite intentionally, since these two words really don't exist in the analytic situation.) As already mentioned, the small number of objective expressions (writing, painting, etc.) is not great enough to exclude the possibility that here something was evoked by the fact of analysis. To be sure, it is unquestionable that the fairy tales referred to played a certain role in the patients' childhood, for otherwise they would scarcely have been in a position to retrieve the content in part or even in toto from memory. But whether precisely this fairy tale told me in analysis was the same tale that alone was fascinating for the entire period of childhood seems to me more than doubtful. When one observes children, one sees that the fairy tales change, but not the basic problems, and when changes occur, a similar tale is chosen. But it would also be entirely possible that the favorite fairy tale suffers the same fate as early childhood memories. When Freud formulated his trauma theory, he really still fully believed that the terrible sexual traumata that his patients recounted to him from their childhood corresponded to empirical reality. Hence it was a severe blow to him and brought about a modification in psychoanalytic theory when he had to recognize that he was dealing with fantasy products. Nevertheless we still ascribe great value to early infantile fantasy products, and quite independently of external reality they represent an objective psychic reality in which are rooted the central processes of neurosis. Thus, ultimately it is not even so important analytically that the favorite fairy tale really be rooted in the external reality of childhood; rather it is of central importance that the fairy tale embrace the magical-mythological background of the collective unconscious and hence the central symbology of the patient's complexes. Speaking in favor of this viewpoint is also the fact of the uncommonly great individuality of the tales referred to. Over a fifteen-year period, I examined and treated more than one hundred patients who had a favorite fairy tale. A compilation made in Spring 1974 (Dieckmann, 1975) revealed that seventy patients cited forty-nine different favorite tales, so that one is almost inclined to say that most patients have their own, private favorite fairy tale, and that in spite of the collective nature of this material, the individuals assert themselves in the choice of their own tale.

J. Gebser (1984) has pointed out that phylogenetically and ontogenetically certain realms have played a far-reaching role in the development of human consciousness, realms continuing to exist alongside or beneath rational consciousness and which are co-determinative, especially for creative persons. Particularly of importance to us in this context are the phases of magical and of mythical thinking which E. Neumann (1973b) included in his conception of the ego development of the child. For Gebser the first and earliest developmental level of consciousness is the magical, in which consciousness seeks to free itself from participation in surrounding nature by exercise of the power principle. Magic is, with its enchantment and its rituals, always directed toward power and seizure of the object and toward subjugation of the forces of nature and command over them. In contrast to this, it is in the mythical phase that an awareness of time initially arises, and with it the cognitive processes. Mythical consciousness, as opposed to the magical, is determined to a far greater extent by intelligible curiosity and seeks to reflect the events in nature as well as its own psychic nature in great symbolic images, which, when their meaning is experienced, lead one to the recognition and knowledge of inner and outer worlds.

Within our unconscious, i.e., beneath our rational consciousness, these early stages, which have been unjustly classified by psychoanalysis as only infantile remnants, are alive and active to a far greater extent than we have generally permitted ourselves to believe. They are, as I pointed out in an earlier work (Dieckmann, 1969), intermixed, and we find an abundance of magical and mythical motifs in dreams and fantasies. I would be of the opinion that the fairy tale is particularly suited to visualizing the libidinal energies of these early levels and thereby to filling out the archetype per se with a specific imago capable of giving a symbolic direction and meaning to the drives and instinctual energies. More clearly than the pure myth, the fairy tale has intermixed magical and mythological elements as corresponds to the level called the collective unconscious, and besides it is more personal, more related to human life than is the myth that is often played out among gods or demigods.

Certainly one can ask the question: What is your favorite myth? But to this one will probably get fewer answers, especially in an age which, following the horrible craziness in which we were inflated with myths, had to become hostile to, or rejecting of, myths. Another reason may be that we are usually unconsciously woven into a living myth to which we are bound with religious intensity, be it Christianity or the new myth of scientific Marxism. Thus reaching back to the fairy tale signifies the more archaic and more primal, which often contains the compensatory elements that consciousness lacks.

Now I would like to present three short case examples that will illustrate only the basic parallels between personality structure, neurosis, and favorite fairy tale. The first is concerned with the patient mentioned earlier with whom I first encountered this phenomenon. The patient was a twenty-two-year-old woman who first consulted me in Spring 1961 for an astasia-abasia syndrome. She also suffered from anxiety attacks, depression, and suicidal ideas (the latter having included a suicide attempt with pills). Initially the patient came to my office in a taxi and with a companion and was temporarily not able to climb a small staircase in my house leading to my consultation room; this meant that the first hours of treatment had to take place in the entrance hall. From the thirtieth analytic hour onward there was a small improvement, and simultaneously the patient complained for a time of shooting pains in her feet and legs. In the sixty-second hour, in connection with a dream, the memory of her favorite fairy tale emerged spontaneously. It was "The Mermaid" by Andersen (1978), already mentioned in the preceding chapter and which I will now discuss in detail.

"The Mermaid"

In this story there lies at the bottom of the ocean the castle of the Sea King whose six daughters are being reared by their grandmother since he has been widowed for a long time. Outside in front of the castle lies a large garden in which each of the six princesses has made her own little garden. That of the youngest daughter is "round like the sun and has only flowers that shine like it does." In the middle next to a weeping willow stands a marble statue of a youth.

Starting when they are fifteen, the princesses may ascend to the surface of the sea and view the ships and the world of mankind, about which their grandmother has told them a lot. In contrast with humans, the sea maidens can live three hundred years in eternal youth, but they do not have an immortal soul and after their death they perish as sea foam. Only if a human grows so fond of one of them that he takes her as his wife and a priest pronounces his blessing over them does the soul of the man flow over into the mermaid and does she become immortal.

When the sisters reached their fifteenth birthday, one after another they rose to the surface of the sea and later below told of their adventures. The youngest, who bore the greatest yearning, must wait the longest; but finally the day is there. Adorned with the royal jewels of six oysters pinched in her fish tail, she ascends. There on the surface of the sea she encounters a festive ship on which a young prince happens to be celebrating his birthday. During the night a storm blows up, the ship is destroyed, and the mermaid saves the unconscious prince. She beds him down on the beach and watches as he is discovered by a girl.

From this time on she is seized by an ardent love for the prince, and again and again she swims into the vicinity of his castle. Finally she decides to swim to the sea witch in order to get something from her that will give her human legs instead of a fish tail. The witch lives in the middle of a horrible forest of polyps and creeping plants that seize and crush to death everything that comes near them. Among other things, there she also sees, to her horror, a dead mermaid that had been caught. But she gets safely through the dangerous forest to the witch, who brews her a magic potion which will transform her fish tail into legs. As the price for such a transformation, the mermaid must give the witch her tongue, and from now on she is robbed of language. Moreover, her legs will hurt at every step, as if pierced by sharp swords. Only the beauty of her movement remains, the ability to perform an especially beautiful and expressive dance that will win her the prince. But if the prince should marry another, she must die on the wedding night.

After the princess has drunk the potion, she finds herself awaking from a swoon on the steps of the palace. The longed-for prince is bending over her, and he also takes her in his arms. But he always treats the mute, strange girl as only a sister.

Just as the witch had predicted, she suffers the most violent pains at every step, yet her dancing enchants everyone at the court. One day the prince tells her that he is supposed to marry the princess of a neighboring land, but he would not do so because he loves the maiden who had found him on the beach and saved him at the time of his shipwreck. The mermaid accompanies him to the neighboring country. There the prince identifies the princess as the girl and he marries her after all. All the mermaid's efforts have been in vain, and on the wedding night, which takes place on board a ship on the homeward voyage, she sits sadly on deck.

Then her sisters appear from the waves and bring her a knife from the witch. If she stabs the prince with it and his blood flows on her legs, they will again turn into a fish tail, and she can live three hundred years as a mermaid. With the knife in her hand she hesitates a long time to kill the sleeping prince, but in the end her love wins out. She casts the knife into the sea and with the first ray of the morning sun throws herself overboard. But now she does not vanish as sea foam but is transformed into a daughter of the air who can, by striving for the good for three hundred years, finally acquire an immortal soul.

Clinical Parallel

First of all, there are a large number of parallels to the symptomatology of my patient. In the fairy tale as in the neurotic symptom, it is the feet that hurt and cause difficulties and concerns. Thus a certain identity exists between this symptom and the prehuman form of the nymph which stands between animal and man. The essence of the nymph, embedded in nature with neither future nor guarantee and who strives to become human, can correspond to an aspect of femininity in the patient that demands to become conscious. Below I will discuss the extent to which this problem is present. This is, moreover, a common mythological motif whose earliest expression, according to Emma Jung (1981), appears in the *Rig Veda*. This unconscious complex, which has a clear relationship to the eros principle and to sexuality (in our fairy tale the frequently occurring number "six" reminds us of this), can, on the one hand, tend towards consciousness and, on the other hand, also flood the ego and draw it into the unconscious, as happens in Goethe's well-known poem, "The Fisher."

In the analysis of the patient, the pains described in the fairy tale also appeared with increasing consciousness and improvement in locomotion. Furthermore, precisely as in the fairy tale, the first thing the patient did when her condition improved was to go dancing enthusiastically. I would like to mention in passing that for a number of other women patients whose favorite fairy tale was likewise Andersen's "Mermaid," there existed the same fascinated turn toward the world of dance. For them dance signified a deep rhythmic union with the vegetative-somatic realm and the ability to have a redeeming form of expression. Just as is done in the fairy tale, so too these women use dance as the personally appropriate form available to them in which to shape and express their unconscious wishes and yearnings.

But if we return to the symptomatology of the patient being discussed here, we can see in the mournfully-toned, unfulfilled yearning that permeates the fairy tale an additional analogy with the patient's depression, and in the mermaid's voluntary decision to die a parallel to the patient's suicidal tendencies and ideas.

Yet more important than these purely external similarities in symptomatology, it seemed to me, was the fact that the archetypal dynamics in the fairy tale revealed clear parallels to the situation that triggered the neurosis and to this patient's genetic history. In the foreground of the fairy-tale plot we have a failed attempt at a relationship to a member of the other sex, an unhappy, one-sided, unrequited love that miscarries because the girl is not able to give verbal expression to her feelings. It is a question of an unsuccessful development of the female ego out of the dominance of the mother archetype in the direction of experiencing its own integrity, i.e., toward forming a relationship to the animus and hence likewise to her own masculine component and to the real man. In the depths of the sea, which is to be equated with the unconscious, the Magna Mater rules in her two manifestations. The one is the bright, positive aspect as the clever, proud grandmother who "showed the greatest concern and love for the little sea princesses, her granddaughters." But alongside this bright side of the archetype stands the dark and demonic aspect, embodied in the sea witch with her clasping and choking magical forest. Transposed to reality, we can easily recognize in this the oppressive and mutilating side of an "overprotective mother."

As long as the ego remains in a state of unconscious containedness, in the infantile paradise of the maternal world, it cannot, like all its sisters, get a soul, that is, become conscious, lead a human life, and have a destiny. It persists in eternal stability and youth until it finally dissolves as froth on the ocean. Only the encounter and coming to terms with the negative side of the Great Mother and the consequent separation from the mother puts the ego in the position to create consciousness, to become human, and to establish a relationship to reality. Only when one has feet can one assume a standpoint on solid ground, a standpoint certainly often painful. The loss of language, with which the princess must pay for this experience, however, is obviously too high to allow her to pursue further individuation unhampered. Language as the probably most important means of human communication, expression, and creativity cannot be replaced by a regressive reversion to bodily movement, and hence she ultimately fails in the world of human beings, albeit not without the consoling prospect of still finding a soul in the world of the daughters of the air. In this resolution of the fairytale plot, the libido again departs reality after the relationship to the man comes to naught. She then flows away into the airy element and the realm of fantasy. It is a very problematic and double-edged solution for a normal human being and corresponds more to a regressive introversion and flight into a dream world. Only for a poet who is in a position to give form to the dream world can this conclusion be valid.

If we now compare the precipitating situation for the neurosis with the fairy tale, we find again another clear analogy here, too: At this time the patient broke out of an extreme domination by her parents for the first time, took up an emotional relationship with a man, and at home succeeded in getting consent to go visit him without her mother accompanying her. The relationship eventually collapsed, probably not least of all because of the realities of the patient herself who, to be sure, was a lively, rather extraverted sort of person, who otherwise, however, could express little of her inner world, indeed spoke scarcely a word about it, and above all did not want to talk about her feelings. "The inability to speak," she said, "is for me one of the funniest things. In our family too it is always that way; nobody says anything. You talk only about work and the people at work, never about anything that touches you personally. I am inhibited and don't know what to do." In this sense she was a girl without a tongue. The encounter with this man led, then, to a pregnancy and the astasia-abasia when, after the baby was born, he refused to marry my patient.

If we compare the personal history of my patient with the events of the fairy tale, we find that the dominant figure in the patient's early development was an "overprotective mother." The patient is an only child. Her parents' marriage was extremely problematic. For a long time, her father was in treatment, sometimes hospitalized, for a manic-depressive illness which commenced with the birth of my patient. Hence from early on the child was to a great extent left only with the relationship with her mother. In her fourth year her parents separated for several years. Mother and daughter were evacuated to the country; the father remained in Berlin. After their return, the father moved away from home, and the parents were supposed to be divorced. But later, when the patient was maybe fourteen or fifteen, her parents reached a reconciliation. Just as in Andersen's fairy tale, so here, too, the father scarcely plays a role during her important developmental period. The mother had pronounced characteristics of compulsive neurosis and anxiety. On the one hand, she fussed over and pampered her daughter, who was never allowed to go anywhere alone and always had to be clean and neat. She was carefully protected and sheltered from ever catching cold; friendships with other children were forbidden. On the other hand they came to blows when the patient strongly protested such coercion or got home only a few minutes late.

In her relationship with her mother, three major phases can be distinguished: the first phase lasted into late puberty, the second exhibited open conflict, the third began with the outbreak of neurosis. The first phase is characterized by an unexpressed ambivalence: On the one hand, her mother is the pampering, caring, loving mother; on the other, she is the grasping sea witch against whom no one can prevail. If one did anything at all, one had to do it secretly. This corresponds in the fairy tale to the figures who have suffered death and captivity in the witch's forest at the bottom of the sea.

Then there follows a phase of open conflict in which the patient rebelled, went out, took up friendships, and was now supported by her mother, sometimes even against her father, who had the same constricting and overprotective characteristics. In the fairy tale this would be the witch's pact with the girl.

The third phase commences with the outbreak of the neurosis, with the patient completely retreating to her mother, who again becomes her best, dearest, and sole friend. She burrows in at home. Even vacation trips were undertaken with her mother so that, on the one hand, she falls into the regressive introversion at the end of the fairy tale, but on the other hand her condition also reveals the features of the beginning where the princess must remain with the mother and swim longingly around the marble statue of the youth. The patient's relationships to the other sex were, as in the story, fully petrified, a cool, smooth marble about which there existed only passive fantasies of yearning for a prince-like man who one day would come and marry her. All of this was depressively colored, which reminds us that next to the marble figure in the fairy tale there stood a weeping willow.

"Caliph Stork"

As a second case example I would like to mention a twenty-year-old young man, who sought analysis because of severe stuttering. In his case, too, there was a markedly clear and striking parallel between a specific situation in his favorite fairy tale and his symptomatology as well as with the situation that caused his symptoms. His favorite tale was "Caliph Stork" by Wilhelm Hauff (1896).

In this fairy tale it is recounted that one day Caliph Chasid of Baghdad and his vizier, Mansor, meet an old peddler from whom they buy a strange powder, including a sheet of paper bearing odd writing. In order to decipher the writing, they had Selim the Learned come and promised him a festive garment if he could translate it. But if he could not, he would get twelve lashes on his cheeks and twenty-five on the soles of his feet because he was unjustifyably calling himself Selim the Learned. Since the script was Latin, he could understand it, and thus the caliph and his vizier learned that whoever sniffed of this powder and said "Mutabor" could turn himself into whatever animal he wanted and would understand the language of the animals. But in this state he must not laugh. If he did, he would forget the magic word that he had to say after bowing three times to the east in order to be changed back into a human being.

Delighted at this opportunity for diversion the caliph and the vizier be-take themselves the next morning to a nearby meadow where they saw a stork just then being approached by another stork. Quickly they transform themselves into storks and eavesdropped on the conversation of the two lady storks. The first one offered the second some delicacies, such as frog legs or lizards, but the second stork declined and related that that evening she would have to dance before her father's guests and still wanted to practice some. Then she did practice her dance, too, and in such a comical way that the caliph and the vizier almost split their sides with laughter. But now they had forgotten the word and stood there despairing, bowing to the east and stammering "Mu . . . mu . . . mu" on the meadow. Finally they gave up and spent the night near the city as storks.

At first great sadness at their disappearance prevailed, but on the fourth day they saw to their horror how the son of the sorcerer Kaschnur, a mortal enemy of the caliph, entered the city as ruler. Like all peoples, here the populace also hailed the victor. Now it became obvious that it was none other than Kaschnur who was the peddler who had sold them the powder in order to destroy them. As the last possibility of rescue they decided to fly to Medina. At the grave of the Prophet they wanted to pray for their human form.

As they were still quite unskilled at flying, they became tired after a while and landed in an old, tumbled-down ruin. Here they heard a plaintive sound. When they investigated it, they discovered an owl crying, who turned out to be none other than the daughter of the king of India. On her, too, the evil Kaschnur had cast a spell. She could only be set free, she told them, if someone desired her as his wife in spite of her ghastly form as a night owl. When, for her part, she had heard the sad story of the caliph, she declared that she could help them. She could show them where they could eavesdrop on the sorcerer and thus learn the forgotten word. Of course, one of them would have to promise to marry her. The caliph took his vizier aside and declared he, the vizier, would have to do it. But the vizier said that he already had a wife at home and moreover he was old. He would rather remain a stork than place himself in the situation at home of returning to his old wife with a young one. And so the caliph himself had to swallow the bitter pill, and the owl lead them both through four passage-ways to a secret chamber. Through a crack in the wall they could eavesdrop on a banquet hall where the sorcerer was carousing with his comrades.

They boasted of their mischievous deeds, and of course the story of the caliph was also told during which the magic word "Mutabor" was pronounced. How happy were those three! Immediately they hurried to the door, bowed three times to the east, and pronounced the word. When the caliph, now a human being again, turned around, he became aware of a marvelously beautiful young maiden, the princess freed from the magic spell, and so his fear that he had bought a questionable pig in a poke came to naught. They hurried to Baghdad, dethroned the sorcerer's son, who had to swallow some of the powder and was now himself turned into a stork and imprisoned in a cage. They also seized the sorcerer in his hiding place and hung him up in the same room in which the owl had languished. And the caliph and his wife lived a long and happy life.

Clinical Parallel

My patient is the son of a self-employed merchant. His symptoms first appeared when he was eleven. At that time while on vacation his parents had become acquainted with another family who likewise had a son, and after returning home they stayed in contact with them. After a time they exchanged wives, that is, both marriages were dissolved and each married the other's former partner, the sons remaining with their mothers. Before this event took place, both boys, who suspected nothing, were sent to a children's home. Only when they were fetched did they find out the true state of affairs which was presented to them as a delightful and perfectly normal thing.

Of course my patient was not at all delighted at the exchange. He had had a very good relationship with his father and described to me very impressively how sad he had been during that early period. Unfortunately he found no understanding in his stepfather and his newly enamoured mother, who even expected him to find this stepfather just as great and magnificent as she herself did. My patient did not like his stepfather; he hated him, and during this first period he attempted to give expression to his feelings. In this he ran up against a strong, moralizing rejection from both parents, and now his stuttering began, especially since his mother was more devoted to the stepfather than to him. We find exactly the same constellation in the fairy tale as in my patient's personal history. Here, too, we have the double pair of father and son: the bright and good pair—caliph and vizier—on the one hand, and on the other, the dark and evil pair —the sorcerer and his son—who attempt to set themselves up in the good pair's place. Just as in the fairy tale my patient in this situation loses what was previously his kingdom by his mother's turning her affection toward his stepfather, for in his mother's first, unhappy marriage he had been the main person.

In the fairy tale we also have the "stuttering" of the caliph and the vizier who have forgotten the word and desperately cry "Mu . . . mu . . . mu" in all directions. These two would correspond to my patient and his real father, the two men rejected by his mother. The stork's ponderous rocking of its head while it walks is also reminiscent in a certain way of the stutterer's convulsive attempts to squeeze out words. Just as in my patient's case, in the fairy tale it is the expression of a forbidden affect which provokes the symptoms or the transformation into an animal mute from the human standpoint. The parallels are yet closer when we consider that the caliph cannot restrain his laughter when he sees a female stork spreading her wings and picturesquely practicing her dance for her lord and master. We can imagine how his enamoured mother may have had a similar appearance in the boy's eyes. And the stork's sadness also corresponds to his sadness.

A few years later my patient discovered some inclination to write and as his first work wrote a novella that he called "The Little Brown Dogs." It begins with the words, "I am a dog," and in it he depicts a dog who has learned human language and carries on conversations with his master, but especially on one theme: "Whoever has the biggest yap gets the most attention." His stepfather was a very able businessman who dominated the conversation at home and in company. It seems to me quite striking that here, as in the fairy tale, he chose the motif of the transformation from human to animal of the figure with whom he identifies.

In both "Caliph Stork" and my patient's difficulties it is a question of coming to terms with the father figure and the problem of the shadow. In the fairy tale this is represented in the figures of the evil sorcerer, Kaschnur, whose son, Mizra, usurps the caliph's authority. In my patient's personal history this corresponds externally to the stepfather and the stepbrother who take the patient's place with his mother and his father, respectively. If we now view the problem at the subjective level, we find an identical situation in the patient's inner world. Structurally he was predominantly an introverted feeling type with strong compulsive traits. His unconscious revealed the concentration of magical-mythological motifs characteristic for this type, while in terms of consciousness he was a harmless, good boy who easily became the victim of the aggression and power struggles of his environment and who caught people's attention only in really inappropriate situations by his high-level resistance and intransigence. But that happened precisely where he wanted to actualize or was guided by his unconscious mythological ideas. His mother and his father likewise displayed a multitude of compulsive characteristics in which compulsive cleanliness and orderliness predominated.

In compulsive neurosis with its ideals of cleanliness we see, of course, a particularly characteristic repression of the dark sides of the personality and of the world of drives which is experienced as dirty, while next to the overly orderly and overly decent, conscious personality a gross shadow problem develops which can be defended against only with effort. This was precisely the picture presented by my patient, who was always praised by everybody around him as an especially well mannered, nice, and good young man. As he told me, he, himself, of course, suspected that he carried within quite powerful dark qualities and his inner world corresponded in no way to the bright appearance he presented. This situation presented itself most impressively in a dream he told me in the seventy-fifth treatment hour.

In this dream, first of all, he is flying toward heaven with his family in white clothes in a huge host of angels. Here people in white and gray clothing are running around; he learns from them that the white are good people who have led an honorable life; the others, in contrast, have had negative characteristics. When he meets a black-haired woman, his own white garment changes into a gray color, and a leader says to him that this woman is a later lover whom he will murder. Everybody looks at him who has changed into a bad person and they want to lynch him. When he tries to escape by descending in an elevator, he is caught by two devils who sink their teeth into his thumb and hang on and whom he can no longer get rid of in spite of all his resistance.

In this dream I would like to point only to the powerful problem of opposites—angel-devil, white-gray, good person-murderer—found in this patient's psyche. In spite of all his efforts at defending himself, he is perpetually threatened with being overwhelmed by his devils. The flying motif too, which, by the way, occurs very frequently in his dreams, appears in the foreground of the fairy tale. Now if we interpret the previously mentioned fairy tale at the subjective level in terms of his difficulties, then his good ego is in constant danger of being overwhelmed by the shadow complex, i.e., by the sorcerer and his son. His good side could then continue to exist only in the world of ideas and fantasies, as symbolized by the angels

"Rapunzel"

In the third example, that of a woman at midlife, a few brief preliminary considerations are appropriate. The formation and development of the personality rest on two great groups of factors: on the given environment into which a child is born and in which it grows up, and on the inherited givens in its nature. Thus, for example, we must assume that there are people in whom, constitutionally determined, there is a particularly high level of activity of the archetypes of the collective unconscious. More simply stated: These persons have a particularly strong unconscious that can manifest in their development as causing illness; because of this, ego-consciousness is not able to develop its customary solidity and stability vis-à-vis the unconscious, so that with even approximately normal environmental conditions a neurosis can appear. As a rule, both groups of factors are at work, and it is more a question of emphasis as to which side has the strongest influence. The favorite fairy tale of a thirty-nine-year-old woman will serve as an example exemplifying such a leitmotif of the personality. She sought analysis less because of a neurotic illness than for information and enrichment of her personality, although we know that behind this wish there usually lie certain difficulties in living. Her favorite was the Grimms' fairy tale "Rapunzel."

In this tale, a man and his wife have wanted a child for a long time. Finally she gets pregnant and is overtaken by a violent desire for the rapunzel, a kind of lettuce, in a witch's garden that lies directly at the back of her house. Her husband steals the lettuce for his wife, but is surprised by the witch and forced to promise to give her the child when it is born as ransom, which the man agrees to in fear. Right after it is born, the witch fetches the little girl, and when she is twelve years old the witch imprisons her in a tower which has only one window high up and no door. Whenever the witch visits the girl, Rapunzel must let down her long golden hair and the witch climbs up it.

Now a king's son who has been out hunting finds himself in the vicinity of the tower and observes the witch climbing up. The next day he tries his luck and climbs up to Rapunzel. They fall in love with each other and decide to flee, and each time the prince comes, he brings a skein of silk with him from which Rapunzel will braid a ladder. But this girl is so boundlessly simple and ignorant of the world that one day she asks the witch why she finds it so much more difficult to pull the witch up on her hair than the young prince. Thus the witch learns of the plot, cuts off the girl's hair, and banishes her to a desert place. She outwits the king's son by letting him climb up the tower on the hair that she has attached to a hook, telling him, "You've lost Rapunzel, you'll never see her again." In his grief, the prince jumps out of the tower, landing in branches that scratch out his eyes. Blind, he now wanders about for years in the world until finally he comes to the desert place where Rapunzel has been living a miserable life with their twins that have meanwhile been born. At their first embrace, two of her tears wet his eyes, whereupon he again can see and leads her home to his kingdom as his wife.

Clinical Parallel

Between the personal history of my patient, the facts of her inner life and problems, and her favorite fairy tale there exist a whole series of very striking correspondences. First of all, she was born of relatively old parents very late in their marriage. This would correspond to the beginning of the fairy tale. From the start she was a child gifted with a strong and lively fantasy, which is to be equated with the strong activity of the unconscious, previously described. In this she was typologically rather more introverted, that is, more attuned to her own inner world than to the environment. To a large extent she lived in fantasies, daydreams, and stories. As soon as she could read, that became her primary occupation, and she lived almost exclusively in books. This native inclination was further reinforced by the anxiousness of her mother, who seldom let her get together with other children and who suspected danger in every type of play. This situation is clearly identical with surrendering the child to the tenacious witch in the fairy tale. Here it stands symbolically for the negative, tenacious side of the fantasy world, and, understood this way, the patient had indeed spent many years of her life in the "magic garden," not taking part in the real world.

When she was twelve years old, a perfect parallel to the fairy tale, her father died. For her that was a very severe and lasting loss, since her closer relationship was with her father. In contrast to her mother who had turned away from the world, he represented a certain equilibrium and, as a man taking part in life, a degree of connectedness to the environment. After her father's death, the patient was at first ill for a long time; she suffered agoraphobia and remained in a continuous extremely close bond with her mother, with whom she also lived until the mother's death. In the fairy tale, the entrapment in the tower, where the only connection with the surrounding world takes place via the "long hair," corresponds to this situation. In the fairy tale, the dream, and the myth, the hair on one's head is a favorite symbol for the power of thoughts, ideas, and fantasies that spring from the head just like hair. The escape that she found from her loneliness and solitude likewise again corresponded to the realm of thought and fantasy: She transferred her entire interest to acquiring education and knowledge and had created for herself a general education in many areas far beyond her station in life.

A few men had also attempted to climb up into her tower; but none of them had reached the goal of winning the maiden. They had all been defeated by her tie to her mother. Usually her mother, who showed distinct grasping and possessive tendencies toward her daughter, had been actively involved in this by making the man loathsome to her. But the prince here is by no means to be understood only as the external man, but rather also as an active part of her own soul that is involved with the world around her. Gradually she had been more and more torn away from this part of her soul and had developed into a taciturn person who always only took in passively. This was expressed in the early part of treatment by her near inability to talk about herself and by long periods of silence.

The death of her mother some ten years prior to commencing treatment further exacerbated her problem. Now she no longer had anyone for whom she could care and be there, and moreover she suffered from severe guilt feelings of a highly irrational sort about her mother's death; these guilt feelings were related to her secret, unconscious wish to be freed from her mother. Now there appeared depressive states that lasted for longer periods of time, states in which life appeared to her desolate, meaningless, and empty. But in contrast to this she was periodically seized by a blind, aimless activity and in this condition had to run away, wander through the streets, or go to some inconsequential movie that did not interest her in the least. The fairy tale personified these states in its two main figures: The depression corresponds to the maiden leading a miserable existence and banished to the desert place by the witch, while her eruptions of aimless activity are represented by the prince wandering blindly about. This condition appeared in her life with the death of her mother, and in the fairy tale, too, there is no more talk of the witch after Rapunzel has entered the desert place. To complete the superabundance of parallels, her first dream in analytic treatment showed, as its central motif, the patient alone in a great wasteland.

In the reality of her life she had actualized her childhood fairy tale exactly up to this point (Rapunzel in the desert place), and basically this also anticipates the subsequent lysis of the treatment insofar as it must be her task again to unite this severed and blindly active part of her psyche with her depressive ego and to restore its sight, i.e., make it conscious.

I would like to point out here in passing that working through the issues of such a favorite fairy tale can be of great therapeutic value in analysis. Becoming conscious of having lived in a myth, and releasing the ego complex from the figure identified with in the fairy tale—the hero and the heroine of the fairy tale—is just as important as understanding all the motifs and figures, especially, at the subjective level, that of the opponent or partner as personifications of one's own unconscious complexes. It has been my experience that the patient's experiencing precisely such meaningful connections between his own issues and the events in the fairy tale is of greater cogency than many other explanations which one can offer interpretively in analysis (Dieckmann, 1968a).

Of course analytic work with this material should not be left entirely up to the patient's spontaneity. One can treat the favorite fairy tale as a means of therapy exactly like an archetypal dream and enrich the individual motifs and figures through amplification. In order to dissolve the identification it is necessary not only to make the patient aware of having identified with a fairy-tale figure but also of the need to understand something of the sense of this figure and its various manifestations in the patient's own personal context. The favorite fairy tale, in contrast to the archetypal dream, usually has the advantage of a considerably higher degree of personal relatedness and proximity to consciousness; hence with it one avoids the danger risked with amplification of causing a break with personal, here-and-now experience. In no analysis has working through the fairy tale taken place intensively in one or more hours in sequence and then disappeared. It has always been the case that either the patient or the analyst could return to it at appropriate times during treatment. This repeated working over, this working through (Adler, 1967), then leads to the patient's gradual insight into the archetypal character of the figure as non-ego and to a differentiation and dissolving of the ego-complex's identification with it. In doing this, the method of "active imagination" (Jung, 1916) has proven very helpful. Many patients spontaneously drew or shaped their problem in clay, and one woman patient even sent me a musical comedy.

Within this process, however, it is therapeutically important not only to release the ego-complex from the identification figure (usually the hero or heroine of the fairy tale), but also—and to a very high degree—to understand at the subject level all the motifs and figures, especially the opponent or the partner, as personifications of one's own unconscious complexes. As an example of this I would like to cite the case of a twenty-four-year-old woman patient whose favorite fairy tale was Grimm's "Jorinda and Joringel." The main character of this tale, next to the young lovers, is a witch who lives in a castle in the middle of a big forest. She could attract game, birds, and people to her, and any man who came within one hundred paces of the castle was compelled to stop and could not move from the spot until she spoke and set him free. Young maidens coming within the circle were changed instantly into birds and were placed in cages.

For a long time in analysis before we knew this fairy tale was the patient's favorite, she told a repeated anxiety dream which she had often had between ages five and ten. In her dream, she told me, "I come into a great forest. Suddenly the branches on the trees grab me and won't let me go. There was a witch who lured me deeper and deeper into the forest and commanded the trees not to let me go."

The parallels between the dream and the fairy-tale figure should be fairly clear. The patient suffered from a major depression. She was an only child and had lost her father very early in the war. Her mother transferred her entire emotional life to the child and sheltered her in an overly anxious and overly protective manner. Additionally, between the ages of six and eight she had had hilar gland tuberculosis, for which she was treated clinically.

Both the dream and the fairy tale clearly depict her hopeless condition as a child. In the witch there appears the negative side of her mother who spoiled her and held her fast (her mother's power drive), as well as the archetypal level which points beyond the personal mother. For this patient there was a second element that held her fast, namely her organic illness. Here the child had to contend with the experience that her own body was a frail instrument that could summon forth severe hindrances to life on its own. And also later in analysis she had to face the problem of not letting herself be bewitched into captivity in a regressive fantasy world (like the

colorful birds in the fairy tale) by the inert *materia* within herself, the archetypal image of great mother nature in her fearful aspect.

In treatment the patient confronted the archetype of the Magna Mater in
its entrapping and regressive aspect both in her own unconscious and in its
projected forms in the environment. Again and again in her pictures in the
course of this process the symbol of the colorful bird from the fairy tale and
its captivity by the witch occurred until finally she was able to develop it
into a prospective-creative activity of her fantasy. Withdrawing the projec-
tions of these figures from the environment, experiencing them as parts of
one's own non-ego, very often succeeds most convincingly when therapeutically working through the favorite fairy tale.

Before we take up the problem of cruelty in the fairy tale in the next
chapter, which also contains a thorough description of a favorite fairy tale,
it is well briefly to say something about the frequency and the distribution
of choices of these fairy tales according to psychological type. In my compilation from the year 1975, I was able to ascertain that of eighty-five
completed long-term therapies, seventy patients (85%) spoke of a favorite
fairy tale. This number is unexpectedly high, and I already pointed out
how significant these background complexes are. I found that, typologically, the percentage of extraverts who could not recall a favorite fairy
tale was higher than the percentage of introverts. Among those strongly
extraverted, the real object played a major role. Extraverts are not so dependent on inner experiences, which results in a corresponding increase in
extraverted patients who cannot recall a favorite fairy tale. On the other
hand, the more or less introverted obviously early on have need of preliminary experiments in the inner world in order to pave the way for a relationship to it since external real objects are more highly anxiety-cathected for
them. Additionally there is the factor of irrationality. It is striking how many
patients with favorite fairy tales had irrational leaning functions (sensation
or intuition) and how many lacking favorite fairy tales had rational leaning
functions (thinking or feeling). It appears that a certain openness for the irrational side of the world and one's own psyche also encourages one to
find a favorite fairy tale.

The variety of fairy tales was also astonishingly high. The seventy patients indicated a total of forty-nine different tales, which would speak for a
strong individual factor. At the outset of my investigations, I had expected
to encounter clusterings around the more common tales such as "Hansel
and Gretel," "Little Red Riding Hood," etc. But this, as Wittgenstein's

(1955) investigations show, is only the case when one asks for such a tale when taking the patient's anamnesis or during the very first treatment hours. Usually then the most common fairy tales occur to patients, while the real favorite is no longer repressed and comes into consciousness only in the further course of the therapeutic process. Thus our indwelling human *principium individuationis* asserts itself also in the great variety of fairy tales.

As already mentioned in Chapter 2, fairy tales are relatively unspecific in regard to function type. As a rule, a person identifies by way of the leading function—be it thinking, feeling, intuition, or sensation—with the hero or heroine of the tale. Sometimes, however, there are identifications via the inferior function. The situation is different in the case of "fairy tales" by known authors, such as in the examples by Andersen or Hauff discussed here. These tales are preferred by definite types, specifically by those whose typology is given form in the author's work. Thus, for example in Andersen's tale, one can scarcely overlook the fact that introversion, feeling, and intuition occupy the foreground. Correspondingly his tales are preferred as favorites by persons for whom these are leading functions. Andersen tends, for example, to devalue thinking, as in "The Snow Queen," and feeling, as in "Thumbelina," and hence these tales also appeal less to thinking and feeling types.

CHAPTER **6**

Cruelty in Fairy Tales

In the large majority of all fairy tales we find the extremely complex phenomenon of "cruelty." Already in the oldest known fairy tale of our cultural area, the ancient Egyptian fairy tale of the brothers, dating from the 19th dynasty, i.e., about 1200 B.C. (the D'Orbiney papyrus in the British Museum) (Brunner-Traut, 1963), we find the motifs of murder, self-castration, slaughter, and dismemberment. If we review Grimms' fairy tales (Manheim, trans., 1983) from this viewpoint, they teem with the most loathsome, terrifying, and repugnant deeds that only a sadistic brain could contrive. Thus, for example, in "Little Red Riding Hood" people are devoured by wild animals; in "Rapunzel" children are to be abducted; in "Faithful John" a man is turned to stone; in "Cinderella" eyes are picked out and feet cut shorter; in "Mother Holle" a girl is tarred; in "Hansel and Gretel" and in "Little Brother, Little Sister" people are to be burned as well as torn apart by wild animals. Things are yet more horrible in "Fowler's Fowl," where young girls are chopped to bits; in "Frau Trude" where a small child is burned alive; and the fairy tale "The Juniper Tree" attains the highest degree of horror when a child is beheaded, chopped to pieces, cooked, and finally eaten by his unsuspecting father.

Considering such a catalogue, it really is not surprising that again and again there have been attempts to banish the fairy tale entirely from the nursery or at least, if that were not possible, to cleanse it of its cruelties and present it to children in its cleaned up form. Strangely, such endeavors have never been successful. Again and again they failed because the children themselves found these cleaned-up versions completely uninteresting; they eagerly took up the archaic-cruel original text insofar as they could get it.

In this connection I would like to report a really quite impressive and thought-provoking story which J. Bilz relates (1961). She tells of a two-and-one-half-year-old girl in the first phase of defiance who was given a picture of Little Red Riding Hood and the wolf while shopping. In the picture you could see the wolf, dressed in grandma's nightgown and nightcap, waiting for Little Red Riding Hood. The little girl, who knew the fairy tale only up to the point where the wolf and Little Red Riding Hood meet in the woods, now wanted to know why the wolf was lying in bed. With rapt attention the child listened to the conversation between the wolf and Little Red Riding Hood. The dialogue between Little Red Riding Hood and the wolf had to be told probably a dozen times. The following nights the child slept restlessly; she awoke and spoke of being afraid of the bad wolf. The only—and probably best—way the parents were able to help the child was by finding the picture, cutting out the wolf, and burning it. Now the child was calmer at night, but during the day it often asked with interest about the wolf. Each time it was told that the wolf had been burned up and that there weren't any wolves at all, only far away in Russia. A few weeks after these events had taken place, the child's father wanted to take her to the near-by woods with him for a walk. The concerned mother said to the child as she was getting ready for the walk, "Now you're going with Papa to the woods to see the little bunnies." The little girl left radiant. Yet on the steps an older dweller in the building met the pair. As he passed he asked the little girl where she was going. To everyone's great surprise, she answered, determinedly and without hesitation, "To the woods, to 'Ussia!"

Bilz correctly points out that even this sensitive child sought out the confrontation with the frightening, overpowering wolf on her own initiative. The child apparently has at its disposal powers which must find and confront the child-eating monster.

It is interesting that this child spontaneously seeks out a series of events which we find in ritualized form in the initiation rites of primal cultures where they obviously proceed from the recognition that maturation takes place only through the experience of suffering, pain, and torture. The next higher maturational level can be reached only after the dissolution and destruction of the previous one. The puberty initiations of primal cultures inflict real pain on the initiant and likewise have at their disposal a catalogue of cruel acts incomprehensible to us. On the other hand, in the higher forms of such initiation rites—which, as is well known, can reach up to the highest spiritual processes—these acts of cruelty appear only in symbolic form. But as images they reveal absolutely the same character that we know from fairy tales or from primitive rites. As an example of this I refer to a shamanistic initiation that Eliade (1964) describes, and to Jung's interpretation of the "Visions of Zosimos" (1976), which are concerned with a mystic initiation. Eliade reports that in Malekula the first phase of the initiation of a medicine man takes place in the following manner.

Eliade

From the "Visions of Zosimos" I want to cite only one passage which seems meaningful in our context. The text reads:

> For there came one in haste at early morning, who overpowered me, and pierced me through with the sword, and dismembered me in accordance with the rule of harmony. And he drew off the skin of my head with the sword, which he wielded with strength, and mingled the bone with the pieces of flesh, and caused them to be burned upon the fire of the art, till I perceived by the transformation of the body that I had become spirit. And that is my unendurable torment. (1976, p. 60)

Zosimos of Panapolis, one of the most important alchemists and gnostics of the third century, tells of an obviously deeply experienced vision that came to him and from which the quotation is taken. In the cruel actions depicted here the character of the spiritual transformation process becomes especially clear. Commenting on this, Jung writes that the dramatization shows how the divine process is revealed within the reach of human comprehension, and how man experiences divine change, that is, as punishment, torture, death, and transformation.

I am aware that the phenomenon of cruelty, itself only a partial aspect of the problem of aggression, is something very complex. If I emphasize one aspect, that of intrapsychic change and maturation and attempt to understand the corresponding images from this viewpoint, I am fully aware of the fragmentary character of my investigation.

In another place (1966a) I have pointed out that one of the psychological meanings of the fairy tale for the child lies in the child's having to learn to come to terms with the deep instinctive and drive-like givens of its own nature, and having to maintain its ego vis-à-vis these often superior powers. In this task fairy tales offer the child in imagistic, symbolic form typical possibilities and models for winning the battle. Here belong obviously not only the victorious and unscathed conquest or outsmarting of demoniacally superior powers that appear as dragons, witches, monsters, devils, giants, or malevolent dwarfs, but also the experiences of torture, death, and transformation that we have already mentioned. Hence cruelty appears not only as punishment for evil or for carelessness and naiveté, but also as part of the motif of enduring the heroic itself.

If we regard the fairy tale as an intrapsychic drama, then all the persons, actions, animals, places, and symbols appearing in the fairy tale represent intrapsychic stirrings, impulses, attitudes, modes of experience, and strivings (1966b). The hero or figure chosen by child, who has the freedom to identify with either the male or female main character, would then take the place of the ego-complex. The experience of torture, suffering, or even death and resurrection in the course of maturation happens not only to the hero or heroine of the fairy tale, and not only, as in "Hansel and Gretel," to the evil adversary. Admittedly both these figures also suffer before they are set free. The same thing takes place in "Little Brother, Little Sister," where the brother is transformed and the sister smothers in the bathroom; Little Red Riding Hood is swallowed; and the boy in "The Juniper Tree" is even dismembered and devoured. But practically everywhere death is followed by resurrection, which is expressed in symbolic language as the successful attainment of the next-higher level of maturation.

Now in spite of the evidence of analogies in initiation rites, or in a series of gnostic or alchemical symbols, it is to some degree speculative to presume maturational and developmental events behind fairy-tale symbols if we cannot find corresponding proof for them in case materials. It is necessary that the same images and symbols that occur in fairy tales also appear in the dreams and fantasies that accompany emotional maturational processes, and that a clear relationship among both fairy-tale symbols and dream and fantasy images be established.

"The Girl Without Hands"

Here I would like to report such a parallel from an analysis. It was the case of a twenty-four-year-old woman who sought treatment because of a severe neurosis, predominantly with anxiety, compulsive behaviors, and gall bladder and stomach symptoms. Additionally, there were suicidal tendencies with manifest suicide attempts and addiction to medications.

In the 104th analytic hour the patient had the following dream:

> I was with a friend in a hotel. It was night. Several people came who wanted to speak with the proprietor of the hotel. I opened the door, but my woman friend wasn't there. I let the people in, and they said to me that the friend, who was now my sister, was dead. She had been run over. I cried. My father was in another room, and he looked just like my present boyfriend. He told me it was nonsense.
>
> Then I found myself in a gigantic building with many rooms. I said to the people there that my divorced husband, who was locked up there, had to be let out, and they had to lock me up instead. In the attic there was a person who said that if I went to the cellar and let somebody cut off my hands, then I could go to him. I went to the cellar and a man with a knife cut my hands off. I cried and then was taken up and let in to see him.

After the patient had told this dream, she vaguely remembered that there was some fairy tale in which a girl's hands are chopped off. This very tale had been her favorite in her early childhood. We then determined that it was the Grimms' tale of "The Girl Without Hands."

Now I would like to investigate particularly, both in the patient's dream and in the fairy tale, the cruel chopping off of the hands and attempt to grasp the profound significance and the meaning in this image for the experience and development of this patient. But first the content of the fairy tale will be reviewed in summary form.

> A poor miller who owned nothing but his mill and an apple tree standing behind it went one day into the forest for wood and met an old man there. The old man promised him riches if he would give him what stood behind the mill. The miller assumed that only the old apple tree was there, and agreed to the bargain; and when he got home, he found the cabinets and chests full. But when his wife learned of the bargain she cried out in horror that it must have been the devil who had had in mind not the apple tree but the daughter, who had been standing behind the mill sweeping the yard.

When the appointed time arrived and the evil one came to fetch her, she washed herself clean and with chalk made a circle around herself so that the devil could not approach her. Angrily he demanded from the miller that all water be kept from her, because if she was allowed to wash, he would have no power over her. But when the devil returned the next morning, she had cried on her hands, and again he could not approach her. Then in a rage he demanded that the miller chop off her hands, lest the devil fetch the miller in her stead. So the miller finally cut off his daughter's hands. When the devil arrived the third time, the girl had cried so long and so much on the stumps that they were again clean. The devil had to withdraw, and had lost all rights over her.

But she decided to go away and walked the entire day until night fell and she came to a king's garden. An angel helped her cross a body of water that surrounded the garden; and there, right from the tree, she ate one of the beautiful pears that was in the garden. A gardener who had seen her eating reported what he had seen to the king, who now, along with a priest, watched in the garden the next night in order to see this strange sight. Around midnight the girl appeared, approached the tree, and again ate a pear directly from the tree. Now the king addressed her, took her with him into the royal castle, and because she was so beautiful and devout, he took her as his wife and had silver hands made for her.

After a year the king had to go on a campaign and left his young wife in the care of his mother. During this time the queen bore a child, and the king's mother quickly wrote the news to her son. But while the messenger napped by a brook, the devil exchanged the letters, and so the king read that his wife had given birth to a changeling. Nevertheless he replied that they should take good care of her and attend to her until his arrival. Again the messenger fell asleep on his way back, and the devil exchanged the letters so that now the king's mother received the command to kill the queen along with her child, and as proof to preserve the queen's tongue and eyes.

But his mother felt sorry for the young woman; she cut out a doe's tongue and eyes and sent the queen and her child into the wide world. She came to a great, wild forest where she prayed to God.

Again an angel of the Lord appeared to her and led her to a small house. Seven years she remained in this house in the company of the angel, and, because of her devotion, through God's grace her severed hands grew back.

When the king finally returned home again from the wars, he asked to see his wife and child, only to learn the whole story of the exchanged letters. Thereupon he made ready to set out and said: "I will go as far as the sky is blue and take neither food nor drink until I find my dear wife and child." For seven years he wandered, sought everywhere, and finally came to a great forest and in it found the little house in which his wife and son dwelt. Here they now found each other again joyfully.

In this fairy tale the heroine experiences and suffers a series of terrible cruelties. First of all her father's careless dealings threatened to deliver her totally to the evil principle, personified in the figure of the devil, and hence cost her her human soul. Although she averts this outcome, it is at the cost of sacrificing both her hands, which her evil-obsessed father chops off. In the marriage she then enters, evil again intrudes, destroys this relationship, and threatens both her and her child with murder. Finally, she must submit to years of exile in the solitude of a forest, which ultimately does not have a destructive but a healing character.

The point of departure in this fairy tale is the daughter's extreme bond to the father, a difficulty which triggers the developmental process. According to good old patriarchal custom the daughter is, for all practical purposes, wholly the property of the miller ("Do what you will with me. I am your child"), who can promise her to anyone he wishes, even against her will, as here when he promises her to the devil. If we translate this situation psychologically, in the sense of the subject-level of interpretation, we see that we are dealing with a still-immature and dependent ego that stands under the domination of the collective unconscious. The father as the representative of the prevailing conscious attitude, corresponding to traditional, collective norms, reveals clearly a stupid and materialistic lack of adaptation that lets him fall victim to the shadow, that is, to all his inferior, negative, and evil qualities. His greed for power and libido (the latter symbolized here by the gold) delivers future ego-possibilities as well as his healthy development to the shadow. It is interesting that in other variants of this fairy tale (Russia: "The Handless Maiden" [Löuis of Menar, trans., 1959]; Japan: "The Handless Maiden" [von der Leyen, ed., 1964]; France: "The

Handless Maiden" [von der Leyen & Zaunert, eds., 1923]; Danube area: "The Knight's Armless Wife" [Zaunert, eds., 1958]), the girl is followed not by the devil but by a malicious female figure: stepmother, mother-in-law, her own envious mother, or a female relative. As so often in saga and myth (just think of the devil's grandmother who so often appears), the devil stands here in close relationship to the Great Mother who, repressed by the patriarchy, takes on a malicious and destructive character.

The defense mechanism with which the ego finally evades the shadow inflation is something well known to us from compulsion neuroses: a washing or a purification ceremony. The magical cleanliness, together with the drawing of a white circle, prevents the devil from taking possession of the girl. Nevertheless, the devil does succeed in forcing the loss of the girl's hands, which corresponds symbolically (as H. von Beit [1960] understands it) to a temporary loss of the ability to act and the power to be effective and is equivalent to a paralysis of psychic activity on the differentiated level of manual activity. There follows a regression to the earlier and deeper oral level in which the world can be experienced and taken in only with the mouth or by being fed by others. Erich Neumann has thoroughly investigated the nosological side of this stage and thus the prospective potentials inherent in it (1973b). Here again, however, evil and cruelty have enigmatically brought about the good and meaningful insofar as these events loosen the close bond between father and daughter. Thus a movement toward maturation and development can be initiated. The parent-child relationship—having become sterile and damaging in spite of all material prosperity—is now relinquished in favor of one's own unknown path of destiny. Thus the cruel events in the fairy tale obviously express here in symbolic form the old piece of wisdom that the road to independence and one's own development often leads through painful sacrifice forced by dire circumstances.

We are familiar with such situations that arise out of certain states of delayed separation from the parental imagoes. Here we are fully justified in thinking of the frequently cruel form of separation from the "parents' home" practiced by animals, e.g., throwing young birds out of the nest, or the mother bear's ceremony of separating from her young. (It is most impressive when one sees how a mother bear feigns a dangerous situation, thus chasing her cub up a tree, and then without sounding an "all clear" simply walks away. Often two or three days pass before the poor cub, overpowered by fatigue and hunger, climbs down, anxiously squealing, in order to set out on its own path into the dangerous world.)

If the mill with the apple tree represents the realm of consciousness in which the ego has moved up until now, the royal garden, which she finds in the glow of the moonlight and enters, corresponds to the unconscious. Here an angel comes to her aid, probably the same angel that later appears in the solitude of the forest. As Allenby (n.d.) has demonstrated, we can see in the angel an image of the transcendent function, that function which is capable of bridging the great opposites and which, as here, is able to establish a relationship between the conscious and the unconscious.

Here the animus figure—that is, an independent, non-paternal form of activity, energy, ability to act and to form ideas—meets the girl. For reasons of clarity I will forgo examining in depth all the characters and symbols that appear, insofar as they are not relevant to the case material. Consequently I discuss this section of the fairy tale only briefly. As in so many fairy tales, the first encounter between the ego and the animus does not turn out well for the long run. The simple union of the two lovers is not capable of reestablishing the ego's full ability to act, and the girl must make do with prostheses rather than her own hands. Here there is clearly a condition of identity between the ego and the animus in which the ego must manage by seizing the crutch the animus offers. Of this condition Emma Jung writes:

> In a state of identification with the animus, we think, say, or do something in the full conviction that it is we who are doing it, while in reality, without our having been aware of it, the animus has been speaking through us.
>
> Often it is very difficult to realize that a thought or opinion has been dictated by the animus and is not one's own most particular conviction, because the animus has at its command a sort of aggressive authority and power of suggestion. It derives this authority from its connection with the universal mind, but the force of suggestion it exercises is due to woman's own passivity in thinking and her corresponding lack of critical ability. (1981, p.14)

Obviously in our fairy tale this sort of condition has arisen in which the rigid, lifeless prostheses can represent a symbolic expression also of the nosological side of her dealing with the world and hence correspond to such uncritically accepted general opinions and ideas. And so the seeming harmony, too, is very quickly disrupted again by a conflict which separates the king and the maiden. One suspects, not unjustly, that here again, as in all wars, the devil has his finger in the pie.

Then the child is born and the letters are substituted, corresponding to a falsification of the relationship between the ego and the unconscious (the animus). The mental contents that now rise into consciousness from the unconscious become negative, evil, and demonic because of the shadow aspect that accompanies them, and again they threaten to destroy the ego. But things have taken a small turn for the better, for this time the evil is compensated by a benevolent mother figure rather than by the practice of a cleansing ritual that leads to the amputation of the hands. Opposite the demonic shadow that, as we have seen, is linked with the negative feminine in some deeply enigmatic way, there has now been constellated a benevolent mother figure that is in the position to diminish the degree of destruction without further loss of essential ego functions. Here again evil and cruelty force a painful dissolution of the still-prevailing, unsatisfactory state and force the girl to take a further developmental and maturational step, which finally ends with the restitution of the lost ego functions: Her hands grow back.

The seven years of solitude in the forest, which bring about the real turning point in the action and which we know as a motif from other fairy tales (e.g., "Rapunzel," or in similar form in the "Twelve Brothers" and "The Six Swans"), correspond to a deepened state of introversion, a long, lonely period of being left to one's own resources. Only the transcendental aspect, the angel, is admitted, which probably forms the bridge to the deeper levels of the natural unconscious which must be activated for the necessary healing to take place. Only after this occurs can a final resolution of the relationship to the masculine be undertaken, and the threat to future possibilities, symbolized in the child, is neutralized.

Hedwig von Beit writes:

> This retreat into forest solitude, a religious motif, is the act of a medieval penitent, and in the history of culture it goes back to the ancient anchorite practices in which influences from India played a part. The purpose of such behavior is to bring about the greatest possible degree of introversion and to remove all attachments to the external object. Thus there arises a corresponding enlivening of the inner world, intensified to the point of auditory hallucinations, visions, and states of ecstasy. (1960)

Clinical Parallel

But now let us return to our clinical parallel, the dream example, in which the patient experiences the same cruel fate as does the heroine in the fairy tale. In this young woman's case, too, the same starting point was a very deep father-daughter bond and concurrently a rejection of the mother. She was the older of two daughters, and from early childhood on had been favored by the father who had an exceptionally intimate relationship to her and, for example, had several times traveled with her alone. Corresponding to the father fixation, this patient later married a man who offered her a typical father figure. He was more than twenty years her senior, a business acquaintance of her father's, and had met him through her father. The young patient's marriage had a quite unhappy course. Three years prior to beginning treatment they had separated, but internally she remained very close to this man. At first during the analysis he appeared with characteristics of a demonic, negative father figure with distinctly magical qualities, a terrifying, devilish father who pursued her in dreams in order to destroy her. Just as in the fairy tale, her father had, so to speak, sold her to this man, that is, she had actually been sent by her father to this man and had thus gotten to know him. Just as in the fairy tale, her father was later horrified and disconcerted when this man wanted to have his young, barely seventeen-year-old daughter and got engaged to her against her father's will.

The same situation occurs again in the dream. In the first scene we have a father who frivolously ignores an obviously threatening situation and puts it aside as nonsense (here the deep sibling conflict, undoubtedly constellated by the father, steps into the foreground). Then in the second scene the demonic man appears whom she wants to reach, and so she falls into the fairy-tale situation in which her hands are chopped off.

A further parallel to the initial situation in the fairy tale is found in the patient's symptomatology. Among other things she suffered from a pronounced washing compulsion so that, for example, it took her hours to dust a room because she perpetually had to wash her hands. Now we know that behind this symptom—as was true in this case, too—there are hidden drive impulses, thoughts, and fantasies that consciousness believes are evil and wicked, and of which the patient wants to cleanse herself by means of the washing ceremony. Here, too, the devil is banished through cleanliness, and here, too, the means does not lead to complete success since the patient pays for the purity achieved with a loss of her ability to act. In point of fact, this patient was practically incapable of doing anything. She spent the greatest part of the day in bed or in her cleaning rituals, and let her current boyfriend, who had assumed the identity of the good father, support and feed her, a "handless maiden."

In addition to her loss of ability to act in terms of productively shaping her life, there were, of course, severe eruptions of aggression combined with addictions and self-neglect based on the massive blockages of libido. If we consider the dream's attempted lysis from the prospective viewpoint in comparison to the fairy tale, we see that here the fairy tale suggests a similar path: first, sacrifice of her hands, which would mean giving up her previous infantile-addictive, unchecked activities; second, separation from father; and finally, as a consequence, her own confinement in place of locking up the devil, corresponding to the solitary existence in the fairy tale. I believe it is quite understandable that people long to be locked up when they feel they have lost control over their drives. Their hope is that they can get a grip on themselves and that the drives will no longer break through. Such persons experience deep anxiety that they will be dangers to themselves and to others. Here we do not need to see only a masochistic need for punishment.

The connection between the fate of the patient and the dynamics of the fairy tale is yet closer in that the patient, as did the heroine of the fairy tale, had a child from the marriage. The relationship between her and her child also revealed serious disturbances, which we can understand in a manner similar to the symbolism in the fairy tale. After the divorce, custody of the child—in this case a daughter—was initially given to the patient. Because of her severe pathology, she was not capable of taking care of the child. To a great extent she left it to her ex-husband. On her girl-child she projected her unconscious sibling rivalry toward her younger sister for their father's favor, as well as her strong jealousy of her mother. Early in treatment there often appeared dreams and anxieties about the child in which it was killed, dismembered, or kidnapped. Here we see clearly how the powerful, murderous aggression resulting from the tight father-daughter relationship threatens her relationship to her own daughter. The shadow of the father-daughter bond, represented in the fairy tale as the devil, still threatens the patient's daughter as a mortal danger even after an external separation from her father and her marriage to another man, and threatens to destroy her, too. This is where the patient's above-mentioned suicide fantasies and impulses fit, as well as her severe anxieties of herself being murdered. The close parallels between fairy tale and the patient's inner situation extend even to these details.

The fairy tale can be subdivided into three phases. The first phase treats the interaction of father and daughter and ends with the loss of her hands and her departure from home. The second then embraces the relationship

to the man, the marriage, and the birth of the child, and ends with her ban-
ishment from the king's castle and her renewed pilgrimage. Finally, the
third and last comprises the lysis of the events in the hermitage: the regeneration of her hands and her reunion with the animus figure. If we carry
further the parallels between the inner condition and the outer circumstances of my patient and the fairy-tale events, we can see a parallel to the
third phase of the fairy tale in the patient's starting and continuing analysis.
What the fairy tale expresses in symbolic form as withdrawal into solitude
takes place in analysis as a willed, consciously undertaken process of introversion and hence a coming to terms with her own inner world, which ultimately led to a regeneration of her severely damaged capacity to act.

In what follows I would like to present a dream that can give us a certain
degree of insight into how the patient's psyche began to digest this fairy
tale that had again surfaced; and, referring to the fairy tale, then to say
something about the fundamental problem of "cruelty" and how it is processed. Following the dream presented earlier, I had, during the session,
read the patient the fairy tale that she had long since forgotten and had
pointed out to her that it might well be of some significance for her. The
patient, up until this time very restless and explosively tense, had for the
first time been able to lie listening, calmly relaxed on the couch. She went
home in a quite pensive mood. I regret that the patient's strong emotions
that appeared in my conversation with her defy description. The following
night she dreamed:

> Someone showed me my daughter through a peep hole. She was
> in a chicken egg, and I had to hold it carefully. I only heard her
> chirpy voice inside the shell. Then I was somewhat careless, and
> the egg broke, and she now came out and got to her normal size.

This dream was the first in the entire 105 analytic hours up until that time
in which the child was not most severely threatened, killed, or abducted.

This dream introduced a phase in which the patient gradually began
to find some degree of relationship to her child and to accept it internally
and externally. In this dream the child is given to her, and, translated into
intrapsychic terms, the relationship between her and her child experiences
a process of birth through which it grows from an infantile, "chirpy" condition contained in the eggshell to a normal size. It seems important to me
that her previously existing intense aggression toward the child is present in
the dream to only a quite modest degree. It is expressed in the clumsiness
with which the eggshell is destroyed. But it is actually used as a releaser for

the process of birth. Like many of the mothers with severe blockages of aggression, my patient, too, was not able to defend herself appropriately against her very lively child. Whenever the child visited her for only a few hours she got exhausted because she did practically everything that the child wanted of her. Often she cowered in the corner of the room, crying helplessly because her timid suggestions didn't persuade the child to be a bit quieter. It signified a marked degree of relief and improvement in the relationship between mother and child when, in the course of analysis, she increasingly succeeded in mustering more stability and energy vis-à-vis the child, thereby giving the expansiveness of her lively little girl a limit which was acceptable to both. Meanwhile the patient had also consciously broken the eggshell of romantic ideas about a sweet, charming little creature whom one rears by letting it do whatever it wants.

However, the form of working out aggression cited here is only one facet of the meaning that confronted the patient in the cruel acts and images of the mutilation dream and the fairy tale. In no way does it explain the deep process of transformation which was addressed and released by the dream and the fairy tale. From these points of view, we would have to conceptualize the cruelty inflicted on the girl in the dream and in the fairy tale as pathological auto-aggression lacking any deeper meaning. On the other hand, in his work *Suicide and the Soul* (Hillman, 1964) points out that only

> an animalistic experience of suffering and a complete identification with it
> is the humbling prerequisite for transformation. Despair opens the door
> to the experience of death and is at the same time the prerequisite for res-
> urrection. Life as it previously was, the *status quo ante*, dies when despair
> is born. There is only the moment, such as it is—as a seed of whatever
> may come—if one can wait. Being able to wait is everything.

Here we address a different aspect of the events contained in the knowledge of the primitive initiation rites discussed earlier: Painful death and the destruction of an existing emotional structure are the prerequisites for the beginning of a transformation. In our case considerable inner energies were obviously necessary for this process, a fact to which everyone who has personally experienced such a process of transformation can attest. This also corresponds to the fact that the patient's dream contained only a small measure of aggression.

In this context it seems significant to me to take a look at an idea of Konrad Lorenz's (1970). Lorenz, who assumes a primary aggression drive, sees in modern man "a creature torn from its natural habitat." Since man's in-born action-reaction norms are mutable only in a slow philogenetic tempo as are organic structures, humankind is, so to speak, stuck with a charge of aggression that cannot be discharged. "For a chimpanzee, even for a human being of the neolithic period, it was doubtless valuable and necessary for the preservation of self, family and species that the inner stimulus threshold for aggressive behaviors sufficed for, let us say, two great rage outbreaks per week." For these pent-up and no longer useful energies Lorenz sees ultimately only a discharge to the outside (1966), which within the collective parameters of our culture and our time appears to be the only possibility. In my opinion too little significance is attributed to the capacity for transposition of libido which is present in the developmental and maturational process of the individual. In the concept of a non-specific theory of libido, aggression, too, is nothing other than a charge of energy that can find application when turned inward in the process of giving form to and differentiating the psyche. It is, as G. Adler (1961) points out, an empirical fact that "the primal, not yet unfolded, polarity seems to aim at an empirical unity in which even the negative unconscious has a hidden tendency to integration." This corresponds to the role which we earlier ascribed to the devil as a force pressing for development. The quantity of energy necessary for such processes was discussed already above.

The clearly masochistic component present in the chopping off of the hands can also be seen in a deeper and more constructive aspect. The patient experienced frigidity and severe difficulties in intimacy which, naturally enough, corresponded to the severity of her illness. Here the masochistic tendency can symbolize a deep longing for feminine submission, the attainment of trust in a transpersonal order, a characteristic which is clearly expressed in this fairy-tale figure. With this stance she could then also accept the suffering, loss, and sacrifice that life demanded of her. Precisely these were the characteristics that the patient completely lacked. The unconscious offers them in the dream and in the fairy tale as a compensation to the overly narrow conscious stance. This still-undeveloped possibility of feminine experience appears *in statu nascendi* in the second dream as the daughter who comes out of the egg. The cruel aggression, directed at the ego, then has the profound function of penetrating the rigid structure of the ego complex, of dissolving the existing form of the overly infantile ego no longer adapted to the present situation, and of introducing the necessary transformation.

Using an individual clinical case, I have attempted to show how a meaningful developmental sequence can be hidden behind the cruelty of a fairy-tale motif. It seems to me that from childhood on (as we saw in the example of the little girl who wanted to meet the wolf) human beings have a deep need to confront the cruelty and horror in the world. This does not lie only outside but also inside us. The human being, as a creature of nature, has not only the kind and protective sides of nature but also nature's horrific aspects. On our way to becoming conscious humans, we must be able to meet these sides, too, come to terms with them, and withstand them. The imaginal world of the fairy tale can serve us in this task as a means that does not need to be restricted to childhood. Originally fairy tales were probably not even conceived and written for children, and still today many adults, especially creative persons, feel themselves drawn again and again to let these motifs move them and to give them form. The aspects treated here belong to fairy tales as an essential element that must not be omitted or overlooked.

CHAPTER 7

The Fairy Tale as a Source of Structure in the Process of Emotional Development

There are lots of things in our souls that we cannot express rationally or make comprehensible to another person. Oft times an indefinite longing seems to dwell in us. It can be so feeble that we scarcely notice it or so strong that it clearly influences our moods, frame of mind, and actions. If you ask a person what this mood is actually seeking or where it is tending, often the question cannot be answered at all. Many stirrings and strivings arise in our soul which are indefinite and difficult to grasp and which appear cloudy and still far from consciousness. Everything new, all that we have not yet experienced and not yet lived, that presses up out of the depths of the inner world toward actualization initially has this character. If the individual is concerned with consciousness, he will become acquainted with this unknown thing that is growing in him; if he is concerned not only to know *that* it is, but also to experience *what* it is, then he attempts to give form to the unformed, to speak the unspeakable, and to shape the chaos that is bubbling up. It is a piece of that creative power to give form and shape that dwells within each human being, and with its help the new and unknown must be carried from the realm beyond the known and familiar world into the world we dwell in.

In every thoroughgoing psychotherapeutic treatment that leads to a broadening of consciousness and a transformation of character, these sorts of processes take place. Many patients spontaneously reach for the sketch pad, the paint box, clay, plasticine, or the pen to write poems or stories. Often they also become absorbed in their inner world of images in creative meditation. People engage in these activities for the sake of making their own statement and of giving form to the inner world. As the Swiss psychologist J. Jacobi (n.d.) says:

> Experience shows that as the analytic work penetrates deeper and as more symbolic material appears, the need becomes more pressing somehow to give visible form to those stirrings so difficult to formulate in words. For neither passing over nor repressing unpleasant conditions but only exposing and scrutinizing them can lead toward consciousness and thereby toward relief and liberation.

In these creations and formations the fairy-tale element not infrequently also plays a role. Fairy-tale motifs are represented in picture or sculpture just as we have already seen happen in the case of dreams. Fairy-tale-like events turn up in the course of meditative imagery, or personal fairy tales are invented and written down. It is unimportant whether they are creations of formal beauty or even executed with any artistic talent, or quite unskilled, helpless, and childish attempts. They are, after all, statements and events that take place between only two persons, patient and doctor. Their generally recognized value is unimportant; what alone is important is that something heretofore totally indefinite can be made clear and given visible form. In this way such contents can be brought closer to consciousness. Giving them form is an important aid in therapy. Often it is astonishing how much dammed-up emotional energy is capable of flowing into this activity, and with how much interest, intensity, and liberation it is accompanied in persons who previously have never done this sort of thing. Thus the undertaking itself is of value. It can lead to a freeing from or a relieving of torturous symptoms. But as long as the contents thus represented have not been made conscious and lived through, this liberation from them remains, of course, something temporary. There is also the danger that patients may get stuck in mere representation of fantasy. Then they paint or write instead of living and experiencing, and the greatest quantity produced and the most beautiful and most lively depictions will yield only the knowledge that the patient has fled into a dream world or has been led off into unreal heights.

A patient described this danger very picturesquely in a fairy tale, and thereby at the same time gave a graphic portrayal of her own behavior. For this material I am indebted to a colleague (Hans Lack, M.D., Berlin), with whom I worked through this patient's case. It is the case of a nineteen-year-old girl who sought treatment for, among other things, mutism. Mutism is a relatively uncommon disorder which consists in the patient's inability, with few exceptions, to speak in the presence of other persons. In a certain sense, the patient has lost the power of speech. During the early phase of treatment, this patient only drew pictures. One day, after she had gradually also begun to speak, she wrote the following fairy tale:

> Far up in the North, where the sun shines only a few hours each day, long ago there once lived a man who was a gardener. But his garden resembled none of the many gardens one finds on earth; in this garden there were only sick plants. It was a veritable flower hospital. Here all the plants looked sad and tired; many of them were half dried out; worms had gnawed on others. The flowers held their little heads bowed far down, and only now and then when the gardener came and brought them water, did they open their eyes and look at him gratefully; but speak to him they could not, for the voices of flowers are so delicate and soft that humans cannot hear them.
>
> Every day the gardener planted new flowers, for there were many sick plants in that region, and he brought all that he found into his garden. When they had gotten well again, he transplanted them back where he had found them. Most of the flowers recovered rapidly under his care, for the gardener had the most beautiful place far and wide, and the sun shone bright and warm from heaven; but with some plants it took somewhat longer.
>
> But for the longest time a cornflower stood here; once months ago the gardener had found her half-wilted in a field and had taken her with him. All her companions had long since gotten well, and other sick plants stood in their places; yet the condition of the cornflower always remained the same.
>
> At first, indeed, it had looked as though she, too, would recover rapidly, but then suddenly it was as if she became noticeably worse. "If I only knew what's wrong with her," the gardener often said and looked at her carefully; it seemed to him that the flower looked sadder day by day.
>
> One morning he was again standing beside her; he compared her with the other flowers and found that all his effort and care of her had been in vain. "I've done everything," he said to her impatiently. "I'll still try for a few more days, and if I still don't see any progress, you'll be pulled out."

Horrified, the flower looked at him; of course, she couldn't speak to him. Sad and despairing she remained alone and felt too weak to get well.

During the night, when everything was asleep, the good Flower Fairy, the protectress of all plants, flowers, trees, and shrubs, came to her. "For one night I will give you a voice," she said to the flower. "Appear to the gardener in dream. Perhaps he will hear you." Carefully the Fairy took the flower in her arms, and gently and imperceptibly she floated into the gardener's dreams. Sorrowfully the flower talked to him the whole night, yet it was as though he did not hear her voice.

The following day he came with a great hoe and at the first blow the flower's soul broke. Yet she felt no more pain, she felt free and happy and floated toward heaven. She saw bright clouds, the sun seemed to her larger and warmer than ever, and the face of a beautiful angel was in front of her.

"Where are we flying to?" she asked him. And the angel told her of a great flower heaven far above with God. There, where the sun always shines and the sky is bluer than it ever is on earth. Up there, the angel said, there are no sick flowers, all are healthy and happy. "But how is it," the flower asked the angel, "that there are no sick flowers up there?" The angel smiled. "Tell me about yourself," he said; "tell me why you haven't gotten well, little flower." The cornflower raised her face toward the face of the angel and looked into his warm, kind eyes. "If I had gotten well," she said softly, "I would have had to leave the garden. That happened to all the flowers. But I was so happy there, I was afraid to stand alone again on the big broad field."

Higher and higher the angel soared with the flower. "Look," he said to her, "soon we will be with God; up there you will be in a magnificent garden, and your soul will be happy, for God will love you; that's why there are no sick flowers in heaven."

This girl's favorite fairy tale from childhood was Andersen's "Thumbelina." It is worthwhile to compare Andersen's tale with the patient's story and with her problems. But first of all let us recall the content of this tale.

"Thumbelina"

In this tale by Andersen a woman longs for a child, and from a witch she gets a barley corn out of which a wondrously beautiful tulip grows. When the tulip opens, inside is found a little girl only as large as one's thumb, so she is called Thumbelina. One day she is kidnapped by a toad and is supposed to marry her son. But with the help of the fishes, Thumbelina succeeds in escaping. After a long and dangerous journey in which she must endure a whole series of adventures, she finally arrives, riding on the back of a swallow, in a warm southern land. There in the castle garden a little "angel of the flower" lives in every flower. Thumbelina marries one of their princes. As a wedding gift she gets a pair of wings so that she can fly from blossom to blossom as all the others do.

Unconsciously this girl has taken over some of the motifs from her earlier favorite tale from childhood into her own story. First there is the motif of the flower being. In Thumbelina it is a tulip; in the patient's story, a cornflower. Then there is the fine, scarcely audible, little voice, and the ending of both tales has the motifs of flying and of the angelic being. Now the differences are that in Andersen's story a human or human-like being arises out of the flower, while in the patient's tale the flower itself is humanized, i.e., it receives the gift of language and of human feelings. Thus it remains in a vegetative realm far from consciousness. It is not surprising that she is also not able to establish contact with the gardener-doctor, and that her voice remains inaudible. Thumbelina's voice, in contrast, is clearly audible to those around her, and "she could also sing, oh so fine and sweetly, like had never before been heard." Both man and beast fall in love with her singing. At the close of the tale both figures enter another environment, but Thumbelina remains on this earth and at her wedding herself receives the power to fly, whereas the cornflower is carried away from the earth and into heaven by an angel.

If in both cases we take the flower beings as symbols of the fantasy worlds of the persons concerned, the juxtaposition alone makes clear that the creative fantasy of the poet maintains contact with the world. His stories and tales are heard, regardless of however fine and delicate they may be, and they remain in this world. There are also dangers to be overcome and adventures to be endured, but no persisting in eternal illness with the dangerous wish thereby to coerce the love and care of another person for ever. The patient's fairy tale, in contrast to that of the poet, gives very clear expression to her severely disturbed inner world with her inability to speak and to enter into relationship with other persons, her persevering in illness, and her tendency to flee out of this world into the heavenly realm of fantasy, from which then nothing more enters the outer world. Yet in spite of all this, it is still valuable that by way of the fairy tale she can say something about the strivings and conflicts existing in her. By expressing them she moves them into the realm where treatment is a possibility.

As the next example of the appearance of fairy-tale motifs within the process of psychological change, I would like to cite the images from a patient's meditations. The ability to let images arise within oneself meditatively and to participate actively as they happen is a most complex psychic process which assuredly also presupposes a certain disposition. In any case, not all people succeed even if to a certain degree it can be learned and practiced. This is not a question of "film-strip thinking" in which with closed eyes a series of pictures, as in a film, pass before one, but rather it has to do with a genuine experience in which the ego participates, sensing and suffering with all the qualities of feeling. In analytical psychology it is called "active imagination" (Jung, 1955).

This patient had brought along a dream to his analytic hour in which he and two (male or female) friends found in a meadow a huge, circular glass disk about ten centimeters thick. He was not able to do much with this image, and his associations in the hour did not initially take us very far either. But since this round piece of glass still interested and fascinated him, he decided to meditate on it at home. He brought the following notes to the next hour:

> *Patient Notes:* Twice I began to meditate and concentrated my attention on the disk. The first time it changed into a thick, round block of marble. Then there appeared a scaffolding on which Egyptians were working. They carved an inscription on the block which, however, I could not read. Then it rolled toward a forest in the background, got smaller and smaller, and finally vanished. Then it changed into a great yellow, winged serpent. Then I myself was in the forest, too, and walked around there aimlessly and very excitedly. Then I sat on the serpent and flew with it to Tibet to a cloister. I felt feelings of disgust. I didn't want to stay there and came back. I broke off the meditation and began again.

> This time the disk transformed into the planet earth, which turned slowly, and which I observed at first from a distance. Gradually it

came closer, and I floated down somewhere in Africa. Morning
mist lay over the land; it was a sunny day, and again a dense
forest lay before me. I lay on the ground with my nose to the earth
and saw a large rose chafer [a large beetle]. It started to move,
and I followed it. It led me to a huge cave whose entrance was
covered with stone slabs. As I came closer, they moved aside. I
stepped in and found the great personages of Roman history as-
sembled at a banquet. A man gave me a drink of red wine from a
golden goblet. Then the cave collapsed. Again I was standing in
the field plowing. A wondrously beautiful steer pulled the plow.
After that I sowed wheat. Finally I went with the steer to the river
and we both drank.

This very differentiated man standing on the threshold of midlife was
concerned at this point in time with problems having to do with his ability
to work productively. The round glass disk, which had been found in the
previous dream and had given rise to the meditative process, is reminiscent
of the function of the glass ball in Indian "crystal gazing," which serves as a
"yantra" to make unconscious contents visible. C. A. Meier (1967) reports
a similar dream in which precious stones fulfill this function. In the fairy
tale, the glass reminds us of the mirror in which one can see the entire
world, a symbol known to us from the Greek version of the snake fairy tale
discussed in this book.

Two meditative sequences of images then occur which express a series
of events thoroughly fairy-tale-like in character. In the first a winged serpent carries the patient to a cloister, which obviously does not please him.
He breaks this meditation off. The symbol of the serpent is likewise known
to us from the first fairy tale as an expression of deep instinctive powers.
Here it is also equipped with wings, and this motif, too, occurs in fairy
tales. In the fourth tale in the Arabic fairy-tale cycle, "The Story of the Porter and the Three Ladies" (Dieckmann, 1974), a winged serpent rescues
the heroine from a lonely island on which she is stranded and carries her
back home. The serpent is a benevolent demon who expresses her gratitude for help previously offered her. In the meditation, the winged serpent
corresponds to a strong trend toward introversion in the patient's psychic
energy. The cloister is used as an expression for a place which is completely secluded from the outer world and concentrated on the inner
world. Opinions can differ on whether the patient's decision not to yield to
this instinctive trend was right. Whichever path the patient chooses is al-

ways his decision. Here he obviously fears an overly strong force removing him from the world.

Tibet is very far removed from us, and the Buddhist mysticism's indifference toward *sansara*—the world of appearances—is very difficult for westerners to understand. Presumably the patient did better to seek a connection with the "patterns" of his own culture, as happens in the second meditation. Faust, too, has to renounce his relationship with the Earth Spirit because it exceeds his capacities of comprehension. Visions of too great a magnitude often lead to a psychic inflation in which then downright irresponsible things happen from the other side, for which blessed Niklaus von Flue, who let his wife and children perish in misery, is a good example (von Franz, n.d.).

In the second meditation, now, the patient lands with his nose to the ground, which would signify the exact opposite to the flight into the heights with the serpent. Here he first of all sees the rose chafer, which obviously again represents a guiding instinct and corresponds to the motif of the helpful animals in fairy tales. The rose chafer leads him into the cave that is closed off with stone slabs that yield as he approaches, likewise a common fairy-tale motif.

Hedwig von Beit cites a story of Paulus Diaconus according to which the Franconian (or Burgundian) King Guntram (who died in 593) sits down under a tree in order to rest, as he had gotten tired while out hunting. He lays his head in the lap of his companion, one of his faithful subjects. Suddenly the companion sees a little animal that looks like a snake come out of the king's mouth, sees how it slithers to a little stream of water nearby, and tries in vain to get to the other side. He then draws his sword from the scabbard and lays it across the stream, and thus the little animal gets across. On the other side it vanishes into an opening in a mountain. Then it again comes back across the sword and reenters the king's mouth. When he is again awake, the king tells his vassal he had dreamed that he crossed a river on an iron bridge, gone into a mountain, and there seen a hoard of gold. Now the vassal tells him what he had seen. They dig at that place on the mountain and discover immeasurable treasures (von Beit, 1965, pp. 33ff.). It is quite obvious that here the animal represents a personified part of the soul of the king.

The Romans in the dreamer's cave stand in close relationship to his problem at that time. By profession he is a historian, and the area he was working on at that time was Roman history. Thus here in fantasy the relationship to the area of his professional activity opens up, a relationship heretofore closed off and encapsulated in the unconscious. After he has drunk there and thus established this relationship in himself, the cave again collapses, and he can work the field of his life with the steer, a symbol of male power and strength, and again become fruitfully productive. In the following period in treatment a significant improvement in his symptoms appeared as he understood the content of this fantasy.

The opposition of serpent and steer, according to C. G. Jung (1956), represents an opposition in one's psychic energy. This energy strives not only outward into life and the desire to produce, but also inward in order to bring about a renewal of vitality. In our example the inward path of the serpent is rejected, since obviously an active realization in external life is called for.

Clinical Parallel

I would like to close this book with a fairy tale written by a forty-one-year-old man. He found himself in a violent conflict of feelings which, for him, was not entirely transparent and understandable. This conflict had been going on for several weeks with extreme vehemence and intensity so that in spite of all his efforts it was almost impossible for him to concentrate on his professional work. Now, spontaneously, there arose this fantasy, and he felt that it had to be written down and worked through. Afterwards he experienced a considerable degree of relief. Even if the conflict was not resolved, the huge tension that had hindered him in his work had abated. Characteristics of his personality and of the conflict raging at the time are clearly personified in the figures of the tale, as are also his attempts at resolving the tensions, but without his being clearly aware of this. The idea arose, was worked through, and written down in a very short span of time (about one week). In my opinion, this offers a good conclusion to our journey through the fairy-tale land found in the human soul:

> Once upon a time long, long ago, and even a hundred years before that, there lived a young painter in a village on the sea not far from the great royal city of Zuntrapez. His father had been a blacksmith in the same village, but since the son had not been especially strong in the arms and moreover was gifted with a somewhat dreamy nature, he decided he would rather paint pictures, which he could sell from time to time to the rich people in the city.

He did not earn much this way, and so he dwelt in a simple hut a little ways outside the village, together with his two pets, the raven Jacob and the owl Manda. He had found Jacob one day as a tiny bundle of feathers, anxiously peeping in the forest under a tree, where probably the nest was out of which he had fallen. He had taken him home with him and fed him, and Jacob remained voluntarily and faithfully with him, even after he was grown and could have taken care of himself alone. Manda, the owl, on the other hand, had come to him two or three years later as a fully grown bird. It had happened this way: In the field she had discovered a mouse that was just about to flee under the planks of the house, and she dove for it at full speed. Unfortunately she had not noticed the thin wire of a fence which the painter had put up just a few days earlier, and so the next morning he found her lying before his door with a broken wing. He took her into the house, put a splint on her wing, and cared for her until she was again well. Out of gratitude she now remained with him, too, and so the three of them lived happily and contentedly together in the little house close to the sea.

They understood each other well, for one day by chance an old trunk had been washed up on the shore in which the painter had found some books from the estate of the famous veterinarian Dr. Doolittle, and among them there was a complete lexicon of the language of the birds. Of course the painter studied this diligently, and so he could soon converse with Jacob the raven and Manda the owl. Thus he also learned that Manda was not really called Manda but Amanda. Her crash landing had been so hard that this first, soft vowel had gotten broken out of her name, and all their later searching didn't amount to much; they couldn't find the A again. Manda was quite sad about it, for she had particularly liked the A, and often she stole jealous glances at Jacob to whom this could not have happened, as he had wrapped his two soft and vulnerable vowels carefully between the more stable consonants. But with time she consoled herself since she still had two other A's in her name.

Everything would have gone well with the three of them if the entire land had not been struck by a long-lasting, horrible plague, which came about thus: the king's daughter, the young, beautiful, and charming princess, had, through an incident nobody could explain, lost her shadow and since that time had turned into a really strange creature. She could not tolerate anything at all in the royal palace that had to do with dirt or was not completely neat, and so she ran around the whole day wiping away every speck of dust that she found anywhere. It went so far that once an old servant surprised her in the great coronation hall as she was removing the dust from the fringes of every single one of the many carpets and was lining them up neatly in a row like the soldiers of a bodyguard. But she never got on to any proper work. Indeed, that made her very sad, but she could cry about it as little as she could laugh about it, because that would have disturbed the tidiness of her make-up or her coiffure, for which she needed many hours each day so that each individual hair lay in its proper place. And with her clothes it was such a struggle, too; she could never wear one and the same thing for any length of time because it could, of course, have gotten a little bit dirty. She used up shoes so fast that her father, the old king, had established a royal shoe factory since it would have been far too expensive to buy them all.

Many malicious people in the city—the Social Democrats, for example—really weren't convinced about the dirt, and in whispers they spoke of her as a clothes horse who was proud and had a craving to dominate; but that wasn't true at all. There was no one more modest and humble than she, for she fulfilled every wish of her father and of everybody else she liked, even if it be the worse for her, and never yet had she stuck her tongue out at the old king. Strangely enough, she could not bear the smell of her own body, either, although it was not at all bad, and every morning she had her lady in waiting pour a whole bottle of perfume over her. Many especially sensitive people fainted and had to be carried out if they had been in the same room with her for any length of time. Once the princess shook her head about this, but then she no longer dared to because when she had done so, the seven-hundred-fifty-sixth hair on the left side of her coiffeur had gotten tangled up with the seven-hundred-fifty-eighth, and the lady's maid had needed a full hour to disentangle the two hairs again. Many suitors had come to her and asked for her hand in marriage, but she gave all of them the task of bringing back her shadow, which was supposed to be on a distant island, and they all journeyed off but not a one returned.

Things with the princess were in a bad way, and since she as the young princess and heir of the realm embodied its fertility and growth, the entire land dried up. The fruit trees no longer bore fruit, the heads of grain in the fields were empty and barren, and in place of fat potatoes, there grew only tiny, little roots that nobody could eat.

And so the entire world suffered and sighed, and even the young painter suffered and sighed, for the people in the city no longer bought his pictures because they had to pay a lot of money for grain from abroad. Manda, the owl, felt badly about it, and so she got ready and one night secretly flew to the palace and into the princess's bed chamber because she hoped to find out something there. She was in luck, for the princess had the habit of talking in her sleep, and so Manda learned something the first night. From then on she flew every night to the sleeping princess, and when she had been with her seven nights, she knew the entire story and told it to the young painter.

In the days, Manda related, before she had fallen ill, the princess was a happy young girl who, among other things, had also been very inquisitive. One night when she could not fall asleep, she got up out of her bed and walked through the rooms of the palace. Down in the cellar she had heard a distant noise that sounded as though many people were talking among themselves. Inquisitive as she was, she crept down the cellar stairs and saw rays of light and sounds coming through the cracks in the door of the forbidden room. The grandfather of the old king had had this forbidden room sealed off because it was supposed to be haunted from time to time. In the very early days the kings of Zuntrapez, you see, had not been so cultivated and well-bred as they are today but were rather a race of wild fellows who roamed through the forests in bear skins, drank fearful quantities of barley beer, got into fights, and sported crudely with the maids. You could still see traces of that in the princess's father. These old chaps had a hard time dying, and so on certain nights they still carried on in the castle. But our princess approached the door full of curiosity and peeked through the keyhole, but only a tiny little bit, for the wild carryings on in there really frightened her greatly.

As she was just about to hurry up to her room again, the door flew open and out stepped one of the wildest and most frightening one these fellows, an older man with disheveled beard and wild, bloodshot eyes. In his hand he held a huge, sharp knife, which glistened dangerously in the candlelight coming from the hall. He seized the trembling little princess and cried: "Well, who do we have here?" The little princess was so afraid she couldn't answer and scarcely stammered her name. But scarcely had the Prince of Serpents, for so this man called himself, heard the name, than he broke out in piercing laughter and shouted: "If you don't want me to tell your father everything in the morning about how naughty and inquisitive you were and that you spied on the forbidden room, then you must give me something." "Everything I have I will give you," the princess implored, "and I will go immediately and get you my most favorite doll." The old devil laughed again and shouted at her, "I don't want your doll, you can keep it, but I do want your shadow." "My shadow?" the princess asked. "But how will you get it?" "Like this," he answered, and with his huge knife he simply cut her shadow off in one blow, right at the heel where it begins to separate from the body. Then he again laughed his loud and piercing laugh, took her shadow under his arm, vanished again into the room, and slammed the door behind him.

But the princess crept sadly and ashamed back to her room and from this time onward couldn't ever be happy again. She had terrible fears, for every night the wild fellow appeared again in her dreams and threatened her with his knife so that she awoke bathed in sweat and screaming in terror. "Maybe that's why she uses so much perfume," said Manda, who always thought practically, "because she perspires so much from fear." But she immediately corrected herself and said "transpires," because it simply is not proper for a princess to perspire. "And where did the Prince of Serpents take the princess's shadow?" the painter asked. Manda knew that too, for the princess had once read in an old chronicle that the prince had a dwelling deep under a mountain on an island far away in the sea, and it was to this island that she now sent all the suitors that came to her.

When the young painter had heard this story, his face turned white from rage and anger, for although he had dreamed a lot, he had very violent affects. His blood boiled, his heart pounded so loudly in his breast that the sexton's deaf old widow sitting at her table eating her evening meal two houses away cried out "Come in!" because she believed he had knocked on her door. And so he, too, resolved to sally forth and try his luck at retrieving the princess's shadow.

The next day he betook himself to the court of the king, who looked up somewhat astonished when he caught sight of this odd suitor. He was dressed simply, not in silk and velvet; on his jacket you could see some old specks of paint, and his trousers even had a large patch. He did not promise the princess any additional power or splendor either, and brought with him no riches as gifts; he even asked the old king for travel money and for a third class ticket to the island. Lately, you see, sales of his pictures had gone very badly, and it seemed too shabby to travel as a stowaway. The old king sighed deeply, but since the situation in the land was so serious and none of the previous suitors had returned, he gave the young painter his blessing and the money for the trip third class.

Yet the same afternoon the young painter with his two animals boarded ship in the harbor of Zuntrapez. But before that he went back home briefly, and because he had once read it in a fairy tale and because he was the son of a blacksmith, he forged three iron bands around his heart because he thought that he might have need of them. His heart in his breast still beat so violently full of anger that people in the street turned around to look at him and he considered the iron bands a good idea for this reason, too.

Forty days long they were at sea, sailed through many foreign oceans, and saw strange and unknown coastlines until finally they landed on the island inhabited by the Prince of Serpents along with the shadow princess. Shortly before they landed, Jacob flew out ahead and reconnoitered. Thus the painter learned, even before he set foot on the island, that the shadow princess was living in a little, ornate castle that had been built in a fruitful valley between vineyards and olive orchards. She had a dark, fascinating sort of beauty with full, soft, sensual lips and long, blood-red fingernails. She usually slept until deep into the middle of the day, and generally in contrast to her light sister was terribly lazy, lay around on the couch almost the entire day, smoked heavily scented, sweet cigarettes, and imbibed intoxicating drinks. But on this night, local people said, she vanished into the mountain which the Prince of Snakes inhabited.

But horrible and appalling things had happened to the men and youths who had come to set her free. At first each of them had been very kindly received by her. "Good day, My Beloved," she was accustomed to say; "To what do I owe the honor of your visit?" When he then said to her that he had come to fetch her, she seemed to agree. "But," she said, "only on the night when the year changes can I follow you and leave the island. Stay with me until then and we will find ways to pass the time." So the ignorant suitors simply stayed with her, let her set sweets and goodies before them and drank with her of her intoxicating beverages until they had fallen fascinated victims of her dark beauty. She made them so dumb and blind that they no longer knew what they were doing, and when evening came, she led each one into a richly appointed bed chamber, washed him with salves and spices and promised him that they would lie together and embrace and kiss the entire night long. But then she shoved a rubber doll in bed with the blindly intoxicated man, a doll such as one gives to small babies to play with and that squeaks when one squeezes it hard. She herself vanished and hurried to the Prince of Serpents where she remained until dawn.

For an observer it was a very comical sight to see how the poor suitor lay there the entire night with a rubber doll in his arms, how he hugged and kissed it, caressed it and talked nonsense to it, and each time it squeaked his heart perished in rapture, for he believed he heard words of love and eternal vows. But that was repeated night after night while the dark princess by day showed an entirely different side of herself. She was no longer friendly and charming toward them; the poor things had to run about sweating to fulfill all her wishes. She made them scrub the flagstones in the palace; she had the great coach made ready for pleasure jaunts for herself while they laboriously dug in her garden; and all the errands she had to do she made them take care of as if they were her lackeys.

But when the hour had struck in which a suitor was supposed to lead her home, the night in which the year changed, she then changed him in some still-inexplicable way into an animal. Some of these animals were still running around the island leading a miserable existence; but some had already been fetched home by their worried relatives; and nobody could put an end to this mischief, for the old sorcerer in the mountain was a far-too-powerful man.

She had transformed one prince, for example, into a cock. His whole life long he had craved attention and recognition, had loved pomp and titles, and had been a skirt chaser. There wasn't a maid in the palace who was safe from him. Now he was a cock and as such he still went around crowing magnificently and broke into other people's chicken houses, flirted with the hens, and fought with the other roosters so that the burgomaster's wife finally grabbed him and locked him up in a cage. She was a woman, you see, who had stern views of morality and best of all would have liked to forbid the house flies to copulate. She had changed another prince, still quite young, into a dog, one of that kind with the big floppy ears that always slobber so much, and he lay for many days howling and whining before the door of the little castle, scratching on the threshold and wailing like as to make a stone cry until finally his old mother came and sorrowfully led him away on a leash. Finally, she had changed a third into a drake, and he paddled around in a circle on their little lake, incessantly quacking, and was so much taken up with his quacking that he never got around to looking for his feed, and lived on the few bread crumbs that the princess threw to him from time to time out of boredom.

Such was the state of affairs on the island. After the young painter had received this report from Jacob, he thanked God in heaven that he had struck upon the idea of the iron bands around his heart, for now it would otherwise certainly have burst. But then he fell into a mood of deep reflection and resolved, first of all, under no circumstances to dwell in the castle with the princess and to accept none of her foods and drinks. Thus he remained firm when he stood before her, although her darkly glowing beauty inspired his heart, too, and the three iron bands creaked and groaned, so greatly did his heart expand with yearning. She was very hospit-able to him and promised him, too, that she would go with him on that night when the year changed, and offered him fruits and bev-erages. But he took nothing, explaining that he would prefer to wait. He also refused lodgings in the castle with the excuse that it was, after all, too elegant for him and rented himself a little cottage further down toward the sea, where he waited out the time with his two animals and meanwhile painted diligently.

The princess was astonished and also somewhat annoyed by his behavior, for this way she could not, of course, get him in her power and play her tricks on him. "If you won't come to me," she thought, "then I will have to go to you," and took a shopping bag full of goodies and intoxicating beverages and walked down to his cottage. But however often she went there, it was in vain. Indeed, he was friendly, and they talked with each other, but he took none of her gifts and didn't let her play any tricks on him or let her make him do any menial tasks. At first, of course, she tried, but soon she noticed that there was no point in it, and only now and again did he show her a little attention or do her a favor because he be-lieved that that was proper when dealing with a lady. She wasn't actually a real lady, but the painter didn't distinguish between a real and a false lady, at least not so far as his own behavior was concerned.

Thus the year passed, and when the night in which the old year bid adieu to the new had come, he and his two animals went up to the castle to summon the princess. Admittedly, he was a little bit anxious since he knew what had happened to the others on this night. The princess stood there all dressed up in her most beautiful robes in the great, brightly lighted hall of her castle and in her hands she held a bowl of the most beautiful fruits. She bowed her head to him and said, "My Lord and Master. I will go with you, as fate has decreed, but before we set out, take from the fruits of my garden so that I will see that you are well disposed to me." But the young painter, mindful of the fate of all the others, heeded a warning from Manda, who had seen a spiteful smile in the prin-cess's downturned face, and with his right fist he knocked the bowl out of her hands so that it shattered and the fruits rolled on the ground. The princess's face got white with rage and pain. But the skin of the painter's arm with which he had touched the fruits changed and swine's bristles began to sprout on it. The raven lay his wings over the arm, and instead of changing into a pig's foot the arm became a raven's wing. "Now you can wait another year, you fool!" the princess screamed and transformed herself into a gray wolf that raced out of the hall toward the mountain where the dark Prince of Serpents dwelt. But Manda flew after her, and since she could see so well in the dark, she followed the wolf's path through all the passageways and chambers of the mountain right into the prince's great hall.

He sat there enthroned on a giant crab with fearsome pinchers; a hideous spider as large as a sheep dog squatted at his feet; and the pillars of the hall were living serpents, whose hissing resounded incessantly. The princess, changed into a she-wolf, threw herself at his feet, sobbing, and told him what had happened; but he seized a whip and beat her until she bled, and then shouted at her, "You whore! Haven't I spoiled you and given you everything so that you will lie and deceive and seduce people? Isn't that broad golden band you wear on your right arm and all the furs and beautiful clothes I gave you my reward for your malice? What danger are you getting me into? If ever someone comes who for seven years refuses your poisoned fruits that turn him into an animal, then I will have to die! Work at it, you miserable bitch, and bring him to me next year as a sacrifice, and then you won't have to do anything more and in one month I will give you as many gold pieces as you covet."

Manda had heard enough and flew back to the little cottage on the sea where the painter, whose right arm was now a raven's wing, sat mournfully with Jacob looking out over the sea into the distance. When they had heard what Manda told them, they took hope again and remained another year on the island. Now he painted with his left hand, but that didn't go especially well, and he had to work hard at it. But in her fear the princess came almost every day in new and ever-more-refined clothes; indeed, sometimes she even came without a bra so that her firm young breasts stood out more clearly under her dress or her blouse. And she also brought all the delicacies that the human heart could possibly desire, yet he refused everything and continued to live as before.

The second new year, too, went like the first, only that this time he knocked the bowl to the ground with his left hand, and now this left arm, too, became a raven's wing. Again she changed into a wolf and raced to the Prince of Serpents, who beat her brutally and threatened her, but after she returned and had fallen exhausted into a deep sleep, she had a dream:

She found herself in a great theater; across the stage all the trinkets and tinsel of the carnivals of our vanity paraded. But all the gold and all the jewels, all the furs and state carriages seemed to her empty and hollow, and she left the theater and walked through the night until she came to a fence. Through a gate she came out on the street that lay behind the fence, and there she met the young painter. He looked handsome and worthy of love, and she walked up to him without fear. Then she was suddenly attacked by a great gray wolf, the same one into which this very night she had changed. But the young painter fell on the animal. He fought with it, gouged its eyes out and finally strangled it. Then she was saved.

She awoke with a very happy feeling in her heart, and when the next day she went to the painter's house, she noticed that she had begun to like him.

Henceforth she started to change. Something in her began to help the youth in his work, and she sometimes even succeeded in getting up by nine o'clock and taking the path down to the sea. Now he was really in a bad way, the young man, for both arms were no longer usable. Nevertheless he didn't get totally discouraged. He took his paint brush in his mouth and carefully and slowly with the movements of his head he drew the lines on paper or canvas. Since he again and again had to think of the princess, they were at first only very small, almost rigid doll's faces with an exposed bosom that he drew, and on the point of each breast instead of a nipple he painted a small heart. Perhaps he thought to himself that this place where the feminine becomes fruitful, nurturing, and giving should be, in his princess, somewhat more closely connected with the heart than with her lusts. These figures looked very clumsy, lifeless, and childish, but in them one suspected just a little bit of the colorfulness, richness, and plasticity of his talent.

Thus the years slowly passed. From now on the princess came to his cottage on the sea every day. Her clothes had become simpler but more noble and elegant, her nails were no longer so blood red, and one could see by looking at them that she had even helped the painter tidy up his dwelling and clean it. She also often played on the beach with a little girl from the village, and her delighted squealing when they chased and caught each other floated up to the painter who more and more was turning into a raven. Each year, you see, on New Year's Eve, she again stood before him with the bowl of fruit. The third year he kicked it with his left foot, the fourth year with his right, and both his legs became raven's claws. The fifth year he knocked it out of her hands with his hip and the sixth year with his shoulder. Each time the raven averted the danger of his turning into a clumsy swine, and gave him his own form, so that by the seventh year only his head betrayed his human origin.

But while the painter was being transformed into a raven, the opposite process was taking place in the princess. From year to year it became more difficult for her to turn herself into a wolf at night, and she retained her human form more and more. But since the Prince of Serpents had power only over her wolf's form, he gradually lost his power over her. More and more enraged, helpless, and anxious he stormed about in his cave and began to rip strands of hair out of his own beard.

In Zuntrapez, too, strange things were happening. The old king's daughter ceased lining up the carpet fringes, didn't wash her hands so frightfully often, and sometimes she even sniffed the skin of her own arm pensively, and her own scent seemed not at all so bad to her any more which then also led her to reduce significantly her consumption of perfume, a fact which also greatly benefited the state treasury. She was no longer so overly accommodating and began to say no more often, and once she even dared to contradict the old king, her father, which of course all the newspapers in Zuntrapez reported the next day with ill-concealed, malicious delight.

When New Year's Eve arrived the seventh time, the painter again stood before the princess and looked with sad eyes at the bowl of fruit in her hands. This time doubt seized his heart and he lost courage. His reason told him that on this earth there could not possibly be such a thing as redemption for this princess, and that he was giving up his human form for naught, that there was no answer for him in the wilderness of his longing, and he felt lonely and alone as never before.

Yet there was something in him that was stronger than he was and that moved him to raise his head and ram it into the bowl with all his might. Thus he excluded himself from all human company and became a raven. But at that moment when his human visage turned into that of an animal, the mountain collapsed and the Prince of Serpents died his death. In the harbor, however, lay a ship with unfurled sails which the princess boarded to return home. About its masts three birds circled and accompanied it right up to the coast of Zuntrapez. There sheer joy reigned and all the bells tolled her homecoming, and when they greeted each other with an embrace, the dark and the light princess, they fused again into one, and the lifeless clothes horse turned into a lovely young woman. But the ship—and this is one of the many marvels of the story—had taken not forty but only four days for the journey home.

The night of her homecoming, however, the three animals sat together in the painter's cottage on the back of a chair. Jacob slept, but the raven who had previously been the painter could not sleep, and Manda didn't either because it is customary for owls to be awake at night. "Just why," asked the painter, "has God let me become a raven? Wasn't my job good, wasn't my action honorable and my heart pure?" Manda blinked her eyes and said after a short pause, "I believe you acted against the nature of love. The princess loved you, and you loved her, and nevertheless you always rejected her and her fruits although everything in you desired her. That is inhuman, and that's why you are now a raven." Pensively the painter sharpened his beak on the chair back. "But if I had taken them, I would be a pig now." "So it is," Manda said. "It always happens to you humans that you get into situations where you can't do anything other than turn into pigs or ravens."

Just as she said that the door opened and the princess entered. Her hair was tousled and her hands smelled of earth and even a little bit of manure, for she had just spaded her garden behind the castle so that the land would become fertile. But the painter liked her a lot better than before. She stood in front of him, and as she looked at his animal form, she sensed a feeling in her heart that she had never before known and that humans call sympathy or pity. It got so strong in her that it overcame her hurt pride and she was able to cry. And these tears of forgiveness that dropped on the raven's feathers changed him back into a human being so that they were all happy, and the pictures that he subsequently painted — they, finally, were genuinely his. Remarkably, the long lost A of Manda's name turned up at this moment. It had gotten stuck under one of the iron bands that the painter had around his heart, and nobody knew how it had gotten there. Nobody was happier about it than "A"manda herself.

An attempt at interpreting this story can only touch on the broad outlines without going into the multitude of details. Quite obviously it has to do with a shadow problem. In the psychology of Jung, the term "shadow" designates the personification of those contents which during our life are felt to be inferior or evil and hence are repudiated, repressed, or otherwise not let into consciousness. In their collective aspect they are "the common human, dark side in us, the structural propensity in each human being for the inferior and dark" (Jacobi, 1973). In our fairy tale this shadow is represented by the Prince of Serpents, and the problem he embodies clearly extends over several generations. In point of fact, the family of this man had, already in his grandparents' and parents' generation, established a powerful taboo against sexuality and aggression which exceeded the customary views of the times. Hence a considerable amount of carefree vitality and chthonic energy had been repressed into the unconscious. Psychologically the princess, as the feminine aspect of the narrator, contains his feeling side, which, under the influence of the family situation, had been significantly split off already during his childhood. By letting all dark feelings fall into the unconscious realm of the shadow, there arose in his life a sterile order, which was unproductive and empty, and a fragmentation in his feeling world. The fairy tale develops a way of resolving this problem. The figure of the painter embodies a new side devoted to the muses, which the more rationally oriented man had not lived much at all. It is only from this figure, which naively and undemandingly serves the emanations from the unconscious, that redemption can come. The passivity of the painter-hero whose strength lies primarily in enduring and suffering overpowering forces corresponds to the beginnings of individuation in the second half of life. The path inward as undertaken in this analytic situation lay in experiencing his own darkness, which he encounters following the journey across the sea, i.e., into the unconscious. He must be able to bear all that lies in the dark depths of his own being, he must let it grip him and be transformed by it. Here the transformation is depicted as a gradual blackening and transition into the animal realm. That means that temporarily the ego will be seized by a dark, negative world of ideas. As winged beings, the two birds—the helpful animals—symbolize such ideas or fantasies. On the one hand, as owl and black raven they belong to the nocturnal and dark side of life; but on the other side they are also birds of wisdom. But only he gains knowledge who has also most profoundly experienced the dark side of human nature.

Epilogue

This book differs from the usual books of fairy-tale interpretation in that it is exclusively related to the practical work with patients, with few exceptions (as, for example, the interpretation of "Hansel and Gretel" in Chapter 3). The interpretation of the fairy-tale motifs as well as the interpretation of the favorite fairy tales that turn up again and again are referred, correspondingly, less to the collective meaning of symbols and motifs than to the significance that they have personally and individually for the patient involved. It lies in the nature of psychic complexes that, as Jung has demonstrated in many passages in his works, they have both individual-personal as well as archetypal-collective sides. The former rests on the unique life history of the person involved and on his or her psychic development, which leads to the same symbol, or the same motif, of a fairy tale's having completely different significance for different persons. Since the collective meanings of symbols are also extraordinarily varied, it is always important in the practical involvement with a person's psychic processes of development to discover the meanings that are valid for this one individual human being.

The analytic treatment of a patient is, as everybody knows, very time consuming. It often lasts many hundred hours and extends over a period of years. The interpretations of fairy-tale motifs described in this book have been picked from the extraordinarily extensive material of major analyses. Since the archetypal symbols and figures of fairy tales correspond to the central elements of complexes around which a great many associations circle again and again for a long time in an analysis and which only gradually and with great effort can be brought to consciousness, associations, ideas, images, and fantasies—often in widely separated therapy hours—arise again and again which relate to one specific fairy-tale motif. If one wanted to describe this entire process, one would have to write a separate book for each individual motif of a fairy tale for each individual patient. Consequently in a book like this, some things must, unfortunately, remain incomplete in some instances, since abbreviations or omissions are unavoidable. Certainly the reader will have had the experience, as has the author, of often wishing to have been able to have read in more detail and gone deeper into one or another motif of this or that case history.

Next to the purely technical impossibility of going into the desired depth in an introduction to the practical significance of fairy tales and fairy-tale motifs in analytic psychotherapy that is intended to discuss the entire area of what is possible, we have the additional difficulty of protecting the anonymity of the patients concerned in a book of this sort. Even if they have given me permission to publish this highly confidential material from their analyses—and I would like to thank them once again here—it is still their right not to be personally recognizable in what I have written. Correspondingly everywhere that we are discussing a patient's individual-historical material, omissions and disguises have been necessary, which for the author now and then signify painful gaps.

In spite of all these difficulties, it seems important to me that analysts, especially of C. G. Jung's school, not limit themselves to interpreting the symbolism of the magico-mythological layer of the collective unconscious in its rich collective significance, but rather unite it with clinical material and also include the individual-personal side. Of a symbol one simply cannot say it means this or that. Only from a long, careful analysis of the unconscious including precise knowledge of the analysand's life history and the currently constellated situation as well as the transference and countertransference process is it possible to state what significance a specific archetypal symbol can have for precisely this person.

I am no scholar of fairy tales. I returned to the fairy tale only by way of the fantasy material of my patients after I—like most people—had laid them aside after childhood. The case of the patient whose favorite fairy tale was Andersen's "Mermaid" was the first to draw my attention to the importance of these motifs. Only afterward were my eyes opened to the eminently practical significance that work with such fairy-tale motifs could have in the analyses of my patients if one understood the motifs aright and paid attention to them. Although I occupied myself for a long time with this realm and published many other papers on it, there were still many years and decades in which my interest lay in other areas in analytical psychology and my concern with fairy tales receded. Nevertheless, my interest remained and they continued to appear in many analyses in which they may not have stood in the foreground, but in which they never lost any of their importance. Fairy tales are a wellspring which one often passes by without noticing but which, when one has once discovered it, gushes uninterruptedly and offers its clear, good-tasting water to everyone who is thirsty and wants to drink of it.

Hans Dieckmann

Bibliography

Adler, G. 1961. *The Living Symbol.* London: Routledge & Kegan.

——. 1967. Methods of Treatment in Analytical Psychology. In B. B. Wolman, ed., *Psychoanalytic Techniques.* New York: Basic Books.

Allenby, A. I. n.d. Angels as Archetype and Symbol. In *Der Archetyp. Verhandlungen des 2. internationalen Kongresses für Analytische Psychologie* 1964. Basel and New York: S. Karger Verlag.

Alsdorf, L., ed. and trans. 1952. *Pantschatantra.* Bergen II: Müller and Kiepenheuer Verlag.

Andersen, H. C. 1978. *Hans Andersen: His Classic Fairy Tales.* E. Haugaard, trans. Garden City, N.Y.: Doubleday & Co.

Beit, H. von. 1960. *Symbolik des Märchens,* vols. I–III, 2nd rev. ed. Bern: Francke Verlag.

——. 1965. *Das Märchen.* Bern: Francke Verlag.

Bilz, J. 1961. Märchengeschehen und Reifungsvorgänge unter tiefenpsychologischen Gesichtspunkten. In *Das Märchen und die Phantasie des Kindes.* 2nd ed. Munich: J. A. Barth-Verlag.

Borges, J. L. 1964. *Einhorn, Sphinx und Salamander.* Munich: Carl Hanser Verlag.

Brunner-Traut, E., ed. and trans. 1963. *Altägyptische Märchen.* Düsseldorf and Cologne: Eugen Diederichs Verlag.

Cassirer, E. 1953–57. *The Philosophy of Symbolic Forms,* vols. I–III, R. Manheim, trans. New Haven: Yale University Press.

Chaplin, D. 1930. *Das ärztliche Denken der Hindu.* Leipzig: Astra-Verlag.

Dieckmann, H. 1966a. Der Wert des Märchens für die seelische Entwicklung des Kindes. *Praxis der Kinderpsychologie und Kinderpsychiatrie* 15/2.

―――. 1966b. *Märchen und Träume als Helfer des Menschen*. Stuttgart: A. Bonz Verlag.

―――. 1968a. Das Lieblingsmärchen der Kindheit als therapeutischer Faktor in der Analyse. *Praxis der Kinder psychologie und Kinderpsychiatrie* 17/8.

―――. 1968b. *Probleme der Lebensmitte*. Stuttgart: Adolf Bonz & Co.

―――. 1969. Magie und Mythos im menschlichen Unbewußten. In *Wege zum Menchen* 21:6.

―――. 1974. *Individuation in Märchen aus 1001 Nächte*. Stuttgart: Bonz Verlag.

―――. 1975. Typologische Aspeke im Lieblingsmärchen. In *Analytische Psychologie* 6.

Eliade, M. 1964. *Shamanism: Archaic Techniques of Ecstasy*, W. R. Trask, trans. New York: Bollingen Foundation/Pantheon Books.

Evans-Wentz, W. Y. 1968. *The Tibetan Book of the Great Liberation*. London, Oxford, New York: Oxford University Press.

Franz, M.-L. von. 1955. Bei der schwarzen Frau. Studien zur analytischen Psychologie C. G. Jung. In *Festschrift zum 80: Geburtstag von C. G. Jung*. Zürich: Rascher-Verlag.

―――. 1983. *Shadow and Evil in Fairy Tales*. Dallas: Spring Publications.

―――. n.d. *Die Visionen des Nikolaus von Flüe*. Zürich: Rascher-Verlag.

Freud, S. 1953–74. The Occurrence in Dreams of Material from Fairy Tales. In *The Standard Edition of the Complete Psychological Works of Sigmund Freud*, J. Strachey, trans., vol. 12 (of 24 vols.), pp. 281–87. London: Hogarth Press.

Gebser, J. 1984. *The Ever-Present Origin*, N. Barstad and A. Mickunas, trans. Athens, Ohio: Ohio University Press.

Goethe, J. W. von. n.d. Der Fischer. In *Propyläen-Ausgabe Goethes sämtliche Werke*, vol. 3. Berlin: Propyläen-Verlag.

Harding, E. 1948. *Psychic Energy: Its Source and Goal*. Bollingen Series X. New York: Pantheon Press.

Hauff, W. 1896. *Sämtliche Werke*. Gera: Griesbach-Verlag.

Hertel, J., trans. 1959. *Das Papageienbuch*. Düsseldorf: Eugen Diederichs Verlag.

Hillman, J. 1964. *Suicide and the Soul*. New York: Harper & Row.

Jacobi, J. n.d. Das Religiöse in den Malereien von seelisch Leidenden. In

J. Rudin, ed., *Neurose und Religion.* Olten/Freiburg im Breisgau: Walter-Verlag.

——. 1973. *The Psychology of C. G. Jung.* New Haven: Yale University Press.

Jaffé, A. 1950. *Symbole aus E.T.A. Hoffmanns Märchen "Der Goldene Topf."* In *Psychologische Abhandlungen,* vol. VII. Hildesheim: Gerstenberg Verlag, 1978.

Jung. C. G. 1913. *Psychological Types.* In *Collected Works,* vol. 6. Princeton: Princeton University Press, 1974.

——. 1916. The Transcendent Function. In *Collected Works,* 8:67–91. Princeton: Princeton University Press, 1981.

——. 1955. *Mysterium Coniunctionis.* In *Collected Works,* vol. 14. Princeton: Princeton University Press, 1970.

——. 1956. *Symbols of Transformation.* In *Collected Works,* vol. 5. Princeton: Princeton University Press.

——. 1969. The Stages of Life. In *Collected Works,* 8:387–403. Princeton: Princeton University Press, 1981.

——. 1976. The Visions of Zosimos. In *Collected Works,* 13:57–108. Princeton: Princeton University Press, 1967.

——. 1981. On Psychic Energy. In *Collected Works,* 8:3–66. Princeton: Princeton University Press, 1981.

Jung, E. 1981. *The Anima and the Animus.* Dallas: Spring Publications.

Karlinger, F., ed. 1960. *Inselmärchen des Mittelmeers.* Düsseldorf and Cologne: Eugen Diederichs Verlag.

Keller, W. 1955. *Und die Bibel hat doch Recht.* Düsseldorf: Econ-Verlag.

Koch-Grünberg, T., ed. 1921. *Südamerikanische Indianermärchen.* Jena: Eugen Diederichs Verlag.

Konitzky, G. A., ed. 1963. *Nordamerikanische Indianermärchen.* Düsseldorf and Cologne: Eugen Diederichs Verlag.

Laiblin, W. 1960. Der Wilde Mann. In *Almanach 1960.* Stuttgart: Ernst Klett Verlag.

——. 1961. Der goldene Vogal. In *Almanach 1961.* Stuttgart: Ernst Klett Verlag.

Lattimore, R., trans. 1967. *The Odyssey of Homer.* New York: Harper & Row.

Levy-Bruhl, L. 1966. *The "Soul" of the Primitive,* L. A. Claire, trans. New York: Praeger.

Leyen, F. von der. 1953. *Die Welt der Märchen.* Düsseldorf: Eugen Diederichs Verlag.

————, ed., 1964. Japanische Märchen. In *Märchen der Weltliteratur*. Düsseldorf and Cologne: Eugen Diederichs Verlag.

————, and Zaunert, P., eds. 1922. *Nordische Volksmärchen*, vol. 1. Jena: Eugen Diederichs Verlag.

————, 1923. Französische Volksmärchen. In *Märchen der Weltliteratur*. Jena: Eugen Diedrichs Verlag.

Lorenz, K. 1966. *On Aggression*, M. K. Wilson, trans. New York: Harcourt, Brace & World.

————. 1970. *Studies in Animal and Human Behavior*, R. Martin, trans. Cambridge: Harvard University Press.

Löwis of Menar, A. von, trans. 1959. *Russische Volksmärchen*. Düsseldorf and Cologne: Eugen Diederichs Verlag.

Luethi, M. 1947. *Das europäische Volksmärchen*. Bern: Francke Verlag.

Manheim, R., trans. 1983. *Grimms' Tales for Young and Old*. Garden City, New York: Anchor Press/Doubleday.

Massenbach, S. von. 1985. *Es war einmal. Märchen der Völker*. Baden-Baden: Holle-Verlag.

Meier, C. A. 1967. *Ancient Incubation and Modern Psychotherapy*. Evanston, Ill.: Northwestern University Press.

de la Motte Fouque, F. n.d. *Undine*. J. Dohmke, ed. Leipzig & Vienna.

Neumann, E. 1973a. *Amor and Psyche*, R. Manheim, trans. Princeton: Princeton University Press.

————. 1973b. *The Child: Structure and Dynamics of the Nascent Personality*. New York: G. P. Putnam's Sons. London: Hodder and Stoughton.

Pauli, W. 1952. *Der Einfluß archetypischer Vorstellungen auf die Bildung naturwissenschaftlicher Theorien bei Kepler*. Studien aus dem C. G. Jung Institut, vol. 4. Zürich: Rascher-Verlag.

Rank, O. 1926. *Das Inzestmotiv in Dichtung und Sage*. Leipzig and Vienna: S. Deuticke-Verlag.

Rasmussen, K. 1937. *Die Gabe des Adlers. Eskimo-Märchen aus Alaska*, A. Schmücke, ed. and trans. Frankfurt: Societäts-Verlag.

Ryder, M. E. and W. 1956. *Panchatantra*, A. W. Ryder, trans. Chicago: University of Chicago Press.

Schiller, F. n.d. Die Weltweisen. In *Sämtliche Werke*, vol. 1. Berlin: A. Warschauers-Verlag.

Spitz, R. A. 1965. *The First Year of Life: A Psychoanalytic Study of Normal and Deviant Development of Object Relations*. New York: International Universities Press.

Traxler, H. 1963. *The Truth About Hansel and Gretel.* Frankfurt: Bärmeier & Nickel.

Wittgenstein, O. Graf. 1955. Das Reifungserleben im Märchen. In *Das Kraftfeld des Menschen und Forschers Gustav Richard Heyer. Festschrift zum 65. Geburtstag.* Munich: Kindler Verlag.

Zaunert, P., ed. 1958. *Deutsche Märchen aus dem Donauland.* Düsseldorf and Cologne: Eugen Diederichs Verlag.

———, ed. 1964. *Deutsche Märchen seit Grimm.* Düsseldorf and Cologne: Eugen Diederichs Verlag.

Index

Index of Fairy Tales Retold